SOCIAL ASPECTS OF THE TREATMENT OF THE INSANE

Based on a Study of New York Experience

BY

JACOB A. GOLDBERG, A. M.

SUBMITTED IN PARTIAL FULFILMENT OF THE REQUIREMENTS
FOR THE DEGREE OF DOCTOR OF PHILOSOPHY
IN THE
FACULTY OF POLITICAL SCIENCE
COLUMBIA UNIVERSITY

NEW YORK
1921

SOCIAL ASPECTS OF THE TREATMENT OF THE INSANE

Based on a Study of New York Experience

BY

JACOB A. GOLDBERG, A. M.

SUBMITTED IN PARTIAL FULFILMENT OF THE REQUIREMENTS
FOR THE DEGREE OF DOCTOR OF PHILOSOPHY
IN THE
FACULTY OF POLITICAL SCIENCE
COLUMBIA UNIVERSITY

NEW YORK
1921

To

My Teachers and Friends

STEPHEN S. WISE

AND

SIDNEY E. GOLDSTEIN

PREFACE

THE aim in writing this volume was to supply a needed source to which the layman, the social worker, the general practitioner, and others could refer when considering matters pertaining to the treatment of the insane. Many books have been written on various phases of the problem, but, no one of these books answers the purpose in mind. When the writer first became interested in mental hygiene activities, he sought in vain for any one volume or even for several which would give him a comprehensive understanding of the questions involved in caring for and treating the insane. The facts and their interpretations, as presented in the following pages, are the result of several years of active and intensive work and study of matters relating to the insane. The reason so much emphasis has been placed upon insanity among the Jews is that the material available to the writer dealt largely with this group.

In making a study of this kind, the cooperation of many persons is necessary. The thanks of the writer are extended to Dr. M. B. Heyman, Supt. of Manhattan State Hospital, and to Dr. G. A. Smith, Supt. of Central Islip State Hospital, for permission to consult records in their files; and to Dr. M. S. Gregory, Director Psychopathic Service, Bellevue Hospital, for similar cooperation. For many valuable suggestions I am indebted, among others, to Drs. J. Smith and M. M. Sherman, psychiatrists of the Free Synagogue Mental Hygiene Clinics; to Dr. A. A. Brill, Dr. Bernard Glueck, Dr. H. M. Pollock, Mr. G. H. Hastings, and particularly to Profs. Franklin H. Giddings and Henry R. Seager.

I am above all indebted to Prof. Samuel McCune Lindsay, who has been my guide and friend during the years I have studied at Columbia University, and to Dr. Sidney E. Goldstein, teacher and friend for many years.

JACOB A. GOLDBERG

COLUMBIA UNIVERSITY, Jan. 21, 1921.

TABLE OF CONTENTS

PAGE

CHAPTER I

History of New York's Policy of Caring for the Insane

CHAPTER II

Insanity as a Community Problem

CHAPTER V

Social Treatment of the Insane

PAGE

CHAPTER VI

Recommendations and Conclusion

LIST OF TABLES

CHAPTER I

History of New York's Policy of Caring for the Insane

I. INTRODUCTION

The gradual process of evolution in methods of caring for the insane may be roughly divided into four periods,[1] viz:

1. The era of demoniacal exorcism, or of revenge.
2. The chain and dungeon period, or of indifference.
3. The era of asylums for the insane, or of humanitarianism and empirical treatment.
4. The era of hospitals planned and organized to meet the needs of the various classes of the insane, including psychopathic hospitals for the acutely insane in cities, and colonies for the chronic and mixed classes of insane in the country; or of scientific study, rational treatment and preventive medicine.[2]

These periods, while distinct in their outline, have not shown any sudden break of continuity in the transition from one period to the other. It is difficult, therefore, to fix the time limits of these eras by centuries, and yet we may approximate an historical sequence by assigning the era of demoniacal exorcism to the Middle Ages, the chain and dungeon era to the 17th and 18th centuries, and the era of special asylums to the 19th century, while we reserve for the

[1] Peterson, Frederick, *American Journal of Insanity*, vol. lviii, Nov. 3, 1902, p. 405.

[2] Van Gieson, Ira, *National Conference of Charities and Correction*, 1901, "Public Policy in the Care of the Insane," p. 161.

20th century the distinction of introducing more generally into modern civilization the methods of care and treatment based upon scientific study, rational treatment and, above all, preventive medicine.

The aim of this study being limited to a consideration of the genesis and development of methods in the social care and treatment of the insane in New York State, and of the social aspects of the problem, it is obvious that a discussion of the era of revenge and of the chain and dungeon period would be largely out of place.

II. CARE AND TREATMENT

(a) *Under Commonwealth of New York, 1777-1827.* The first public hospital or asylum in the State of New York, in which the insane received special medical treatment, was the New York City Hospital. This institution was incorporated by royal charter bearing date June 13, 1771,[1] and a building in pursuance of its objects was begun in 1773, which, unfortunately, was destroyed by fire before completion. The intervention of the Revolutionary War, bringing with it financial embarrassments, delayed the progress of the work of contruction, so that, despite pecuniary aid received from the colonial legislature, the edifice was not opened until January, 1791. It was then opened as a general hospital, receiving all cases of disease indiscriminately, and in this way cases of insanity gradually found their way into it.[2] The exact date of the reception of the first case cannot be ascertained, although two are reported as admitted in May, 1797.[3] Hitherto the insane had been

[1] Peterson, Arthur E., and Edwards, Geo. W., *New York as an Eighteenth Century Municipality*, p. 301.

[2] Ordronaux, John, *Lunacy Laws of New York*, p. 199.

[3] Earle, Pliny, *History of the Bloomingdale Asylum for the Insane*, 1848, p. 8.

legally classified among disorderly persons,[1] and were to be disposed of according to the pleasure of the magistrates before whom they were brought, either by being confined, or if strangers, returned to their last legal place of settlement.

Meanwhile, as the insane had greatly multiplied in numbers, and formed an exceptional class whose condition required for its successful treatment such space and isolation as could not be obtained in a general hospital, the governors of the New York Hospital applied to the legislature for assistance to enable them to build a separate structure for this class of patients. This was granted them in 1806,[2] through the enactment of "An Act for the better and more permanent support of the hospital in the City of New York." It provided that the State of New York should appropriate the sum of $12,500 annually for a period of fifty years as a subsidy to the hospital. The new structure was opened in July, 1808.[3] No requirements were stipulated at this time as to the admission of insane patients, but in 1809 a law was passed, granting authority to the overseers of the poor of any city or town in the state to contract with the governors of the New York Hospital for the maintenance and care of any lunatics chargeable to such city or town.[4] This act was the initial step taken by the legislature in the recognition of the insane as a special class of diseased persons, requiring medical care and treatment in institutions of a definite character. It also established the principle of its judicial custody over them as wards, to be protected and supervised in their persons as well as in their estates through the agency of its courts and appointed officers.

At this period there was no institution to which the

[1] *Laws* of 1788, chap. 31.

[2] *Laws* of 1806, chap. 54.

[3] Ordronaux, *op. cit.*, p. 200.

[4] *Laws* of 1809, chap. 90, sec. 3.

criminal insane could be sent, and two cases arose requiring the action of the legislature, the governor not being at that time empowered to grant pardons in such cases. In 1799 one John Pastano was convicted of murder and sentenced to be executed. It transpired that the man was insane. An appeal was made to the legislature to save him and a law was passed pardoning him, on condition that he be kept in prison until he could be returned to his place of legal residence.[1] A similar case arose again in 1816 and was disposed of in the same way, except that arrangements were to be made by the friends or relatives for care in some "lunatic hospital or asylum." [2] In 1816 the society of the New York Hospital was again given authority by law to erect a new building. This was opened for use June, 1821, as the Bloomingdale Asylum for the accommodation of insane persons, and received a further annuity of $10,000, to be continued like the other to 1866.[3]

There was no further legislation dealing with the commitment and care of the insane until 1827, when a law was passed bearing upon the proper provision for the custody of insane persons in jails, and the responsibility of the next of kin to care for or make proper provision for the care of insane persons.[4] It might be well to note at this point that

[1] *Laws* of 1800, chap. 3, entitled "An Act to pardon John Pastano for murder."

[2] *Laws* of 1816, chap. 4.

[3] *Ibid.*, chap. 203.

[4] Laws of 1827, chap. 294, entitled *An Act concerning Lunatics.* Secs. 2, 3 and 4 recite that "no lunatic shall be confined in any prison, gaol or house of correction, or be confined in the same room with any person charged with, or convicted of, any criminal offense. But he shall be sent to the asylum in New York, or to the County poor-house or almshouse, or other place provided for the reception of lunatics by the county superintendents."

Sec. 5 recites that it shall be the duty of the parents or relatives of any lunatic, if able, to support him in such asylum.

during the first half-century of the existence of the commonwealth, viz., from 1777 to the passage of the above law in 1827, the insane were treated as dangerous persons, and the policy was to protect society against their acts of violence by arresting and incarcerating them in jails and prisons with criminals.[1] For nearly twenty years, viz., from 1808 to 1827, the State of New York confined its insane in jails, where they were still treated as criminals and were generally chained, as directed by the law of 1788;[2] in the poor-houses or almshouses, where the chronic insane congregated and were subjected to every possible degree of cruelty and neglect; and in the asylum of the New York Hospital, where they were treated in the most humane manner, by the best class of officers and attendants.[3] It was during the next half century, from 1827 to 1877, that the policy of the state was steadily in the direction of improving the public care of the insane, and especially of insane poor.

(b) *1830-1873.* There was a great want felt at this time for state asylums for the insane. The population of the state had grown to almost 2,000,000 and there were as yet no special facilities provided by the state or county authorities for the care of the insane, other than what has been alluded to in regard to the New York Hospital. The need had become so great that Gov. Throop, in his annual message to the legislature of January, 1830, called its attention to the uncared-for condition of the poor and indigent insane. He referred to the privations and neglect to which these persons were subjected under poor-house regulations, and remarked that "no restoration can be hoped for under such circumstances."[4] Moved by these unanswerable

[1] *American Journal of Insanity*, July, 1883, pp. 50-51.

[2] *Laws* of 1788, chap. 31, sec. 6.

[3] *Amer. Jour. of Ins.*, July, 1886, pp. 61-62.

[4] *Assembly Document* no. 2, Jan. 7, 1830.

arguments in favor of state intervention, the assembly shortly thereafter adopted a resolution that "the standing committee on charitable institutions do inquire into the propriety of making further provision for ameliorating the condition of the insane poor." [1] Upon the recommendation of this committee, there was appointed a special committee to investigate the manner in which the hospital in the city of New York and the asylums connected with it, had disbursed the funds received from the state, and to inquire into the necessity of erecting a new establishment.[2]

The report of this special committee made March 10, 1831,[3] dealt with the causation of insanity, its status in this and other countries, the needs of the insane in the state, and the duty of the state toward them. According to this report, there were at that time (1830) 2,695 insane persons, with but one incorporated asylum at Bloomingdale, containing provision for about 200 patients, and one private asylum at Hudson with accommodations for 50 patients. It was optional for the Bloomingdale Asylum under the law of March 24, 1807, to accept pauper patients, and for this reason there was no provision whatever in the state for the comfortable support and proper treatment of the insane poor.

During the session of 1831 a special legislative committee was again appointed upon this subject and a report submitted; but no legislative action was taken. In the same session (1831) Dr. Samuel White, superintendent of the Hudson Lunatic Asylum, applied for a subsidy in aid of his institution.[4] A special committee on Lunacy Legislation spoke very highly of the Hudson Asylum, and recommended

[1] *Assembly Journal*, Jan. 29, 1830.

[2] *Assembly Document* no. 408, April 14, 1830.

[3] *Ibid.*, 263, March 10, 1831.

[4] *Ibid.*, 305, April 4, 1831.

that county authorities make contracts with Dr. White for the care of the insane but did not advise any subsidy on the part of the state.[1]

In 1832 Gov. Throop in his annual message again reverted to the condition of the pauper insane as one calling for state intervention.[2] A special committee was again appointed and reported in favor of making state provision for the insane.[3] However, no action was taken before the legislature adjourned.

In January 1834, Gov. Marcy recalled the matter to the notice of the legislature.[4] A special committee was again appointed; belief in state provision for the insane was reaffirmed, but no legislation followed.[5]

In 1835 the same program was essentially repeated, with the same result.[6] No action was taken by the legislature to mitigate the existing evils until 1836, when an act was passed authorizing the establishment of the State Lunatic Asylum at Utica.[7] This came about at this time largely as a result of a memorial presented to the legislature by the State Medical Society, asking for the erection of a suitable state asylum for the insane.[8] The asylum at Utica was opened in 1843 and was to provide for the transfer of the most suitable cases from the county poor-houses. In 1850 the law governing admission to the State Lunatic Asylum

[1] *Assembly Document* 305, April 1, 1831.

[2] *Ibid.*, 2, Jan. 3, 1832.

[3] *Ibid.*, 174, Feb. 28, 1832.

[4] *Ibid.*, 3, Jan. 7, 1834.

[5] *Ibid.*, 347, March 29, 1834.

[6] *Ibid.*, 167, Jan. 31, 1835.

[7] *Laws* of 1836, chap. 82, entitled *An Act to authorize the establishment of the New York State Lunatic Asylum.*

[8] *25th Annual Report*, Managers of State Lunatic Asylum at Utica, 1867, pp. 50-51.

was amended so as to restrict the selection of cases, by providing that "no person in indigent circumstances, not a pauper, shall be admitted into the asylum, unless such person shall have become insane within one year next preceding such admission, and county judge must take proof of same." [1] County judges had the power to send indigent insane persons brought before them either to the county poor-house or the State Asylum, as in their judgment might be for the best interests of all concerned. The county superintendents of the poor committed the pauper class.

It was not until 1848 that provision was made for insane criminals, when an act to amend the law regulating county and state prisons was passed, providing that whenever any convict became insane, he was, after examination by the prison inspector, to be transferred to the Utica Asylum.[2] If at the expiration of his sentence he was still insane, the superintendent of the asylum might return him to the charge of the superintendent of the county whence he came. As a result of the steady increase in the number of insane discovered among criminals in the prisons,[3] and of the impossibility of affording them suitable treatment in the hospitals attached to such institutions, further legislation was enacted in 1855. This represented the first effort toward a more systematic classification of the insane, and toward the establishment of a distinction between criminals and non-criminals in relation to their detention in asylums.[4] It being found impracticable to carry this project into operation, and as nothing short of a separate institution would suffice for the contemplated purposes, the legislature

[1] *Laws* of 1850, chap. 282, sec. 2.

[2] *Laws* of 1848, chap. 294, sec. 96.

[3] Ordronaux, *op. cit.*, p. 29.

[4] *Laws* of 1855, chap. 456, entitled *An Act to Provide for Insane Criminals.*

passed an act organizing a special asylum in 1858.[1] The institution thus erected at Auburn for the care of insane convicts provided accommodations for all the criminal insane of the state until 1892, when the Matteawan institution was opened at Fishkill-on-the-Hudson (now Beacon).

Reference should be made to the care of the insane in the metropolitan district—the counties of New York and Kings—where the insane in custody of the poor authorities, increased to such an extent that the almshouse and its attached hospital, both situated on the grounds of the present Bellevue Hospital, were unable to care properly for those under their care. It was not until 1839, when the insane asylum on Blackwell's Island was opened, that any relief was afforded. This was the first institution of its kind erected by the County of New York, and on June 10, 1839, 197 insane persons were removed to it from the almshouse and hospital.[2] From time to time additions were made to the Blackwell's Island institution until 1869, when the authorities sought permission from the legislature to issue bonds for the purpose of raising funds to construct a new insane asylum on Ward's Island.[3] This permission was granted and the new institution was opened in 1871 for male patients removed from Blackwell's Island, the latter being retained for women.

Pauper lunatics in Kings County, as in other counties, had been kept in the poor-house asylum on the county farm at Flatbush. In 1844 the need of better accommodations for

[1] *Laws* of 1858, chap. 130, entitled *An Act to Organize the State Lunatic Asylum for Insane Convicts*, sec. 1 providing that "The building now being erected on the prison grounds at Auburn shall be known and designated as the State Lunatic Asylum for Insane Convicts."

[2] Ordronaux, *op. cit.*, pp. 202-203.

[3] *Laws* of 1869, chap. 56, sec. 1.

this increasing class led to the passage of a law [1] which authorized the county treasurer to raise funds to erect a new insane asylum at Flatbush. The need of additional accommodations led to further enabling legislation in 1851,[2] 1853,[3] 1855,[4] 1860,[5] and 1867.[6] Accommodations were thus provided for about 600 patients.

Like New York and Kings, Monroe County was authorized in 1863 to provide for all its dependent insane and construct a separate and distinct institution from that of the county poor-house, to be known as the Monroe County Asylum at Rochester.[7] Of the other counties in the state, not one made adequate provision for their own insane. There was an increasing disposition on the part of the counties to resume the care of their chronic insane, in many instances, an assumption also of the right of treating acute cases of insanity. This was done by county officers who, on the plea of economy, evaded the law relating to the speedy commitment of recent cases to state asylums, and thus converted the poor-house asylums into institutions for the insane.[8]

Despite the establishment of the State Asylum at Utica, the number of insane in almshouses increased steadily, due to the rapid increase in the population of the state. In 1855 the county superintendents of the poor held a convention at the Utica State Asylum in order to consider what action they should take to remedy the difficulties they were having in providing for their insane. Their recommendations were

[1] *Laws* of 1844, chap. 203.

[2] *Laws* of 1851, chap. 351.

[3] *Laws* of 1853, chap. 255.

[4] *Laws* of 1855, chap. 92.

[5] *Laws* of 1860, chap. 221.

[6] *Laws* of 1867, chap. 546.

[7] *Laws* of 1863, chap. 82, secs. 1-9 inc.

[8] Ordronaux, *op. cit.*, p. 215.

that two additional state institutions should be contructed. At the following session of the legislature a bill was introduced creating two more asylums; it was favorably reported, but the premature adjournment of the legislature arrested its further progress.[1] At last, mainly through the efforts of Miss Dorothea L. Dix and Dr. Sylvester D. Willard, secretary of the State Medical Society, the legislature in 1864 authorized an investigation by Dr. Willard of the condition of the insane in the state.[2] The report was submitted to the legislature in 1865 and dealt at some length with the appalling condition of the insane in the county institutions, and the crowded condition of the state asylum.[3] The result of the report was the establishment of the Willard Asylum for the insane poor of the chronic classes,[4] and the further provision that acute cases were to be sent to the Utica State Hospital. After the completion of the Willard Asylum no more chronic cases were to be sent to the county poor-houses from the Utica institution, but to the Willard Asylum instead. The creation of the distinction between acute and chronic cases persisted until it was finally abolished by the State Care Act of 1890.

Further steps leading to the establishment of other asylums were being taken, and in 1867 a law was passed authorizing the establishment of the Hudson River Asylum at Poughkeepsie.[5] This institution was opened in 1871 for the reception of the so-called acute cases. In 1870 a law

[1] Hurd, Henry W., *Institutional Care of the Insane*, vol. iii, p. 110.

[2] *Laws* of 1864, chap. 418, entitled *An Act in relation to insane persons in poor-houses, insane asylums and other institutions in the State of New York*, the purpose of which was to obtain statistics of the insane.

[3] *Assembly Doc.*, vol. xix, Session of 1865.

[4] *Laws* of 1865, chap. 342.

[5] *Laws* of 1867, chap. 93.

was passed establishing a homeopathic asylum at Middletown, New York,[1] this being the first attempt in the United States to establish such a hospital. It was erected with the aid of private contributions, and received its first patients in 1874. An act to establish the Buffalo State Asylum for the Insane was passed in April, 1870.[2] This institution was officially opened in November, 1880.

(c) *1873-1888.* A turning point in the history of lunacy affairs in New York came as the result of the passage of a law in 1873, whereby the office of the State Commissioner in Lunacy was created.[3] This law also required that private asylums be licensed.[4] It was the duty of the Commissioner in Lunacy to examine into the condition of the insane and idiotic, the management and conduct of the asylums and other institutions for their custody,[5] and to submit a report to the State Board of Charities.

Chapter 571, Laws of 1873, was found to impose exceedingly cumbrous and confused powers upon the Commissioner in Lunacy. Among other things, although he was a state official, instead of reporting his official acts to the legislature, he was required to render a report to the State Board of Charities, at whose direction only such reports could reach the law-making power. Furthermore, in

[1] *Laws* of 1870, chap. 474.

[2] *Ibid.*, chap. 378.

[3] *Laws* of 1873, chap. 571, entitled *An Act further to define the powers and duties of the Board of State Commissioners of Public Charities, and to change the name of the Board to the State Board of Charities.* Sec. 13 created the office of State Commissioner in Lunacy. John Ordronaux, LL.D., professor of medical jurisprudence in the Law School of Columbia College, was appointed to the office.

[4] *Laws* of 1873, chap. 571, sec. 9, requiring that private asylums be licensed by the newly created State Board of Charities.

[5] *Laws* of 1873, chap. 571, sec. 14.

spite of the fact that the office had been established to discover and redress wrongs committed in asylums, no method was provided to do this, as reports had to be submitted, as above noted in a round-about and time-consuming manner. These facts soon became so obvious that the next legislature radically altered the powers and duties of the Commissioner in Lunacy.[1] This was done by the enactment of a law in 1874,[2] based upon recommendations made by the Commissioner in Lunacy, John Ordronaux, and the Attorney-General, Daniel Pratt.[3] Section 1 of this law provided that

> no person should be committed to or confined as a patient in any asylum public or private, or in any institution, home or retreat for the care and treatment of the insane, except upon the certificate of two physicians, under oath, setting forth the insanity of such person. But no person should be held in confinement in any such asylum for more than five days, unless within that time such certificate be approved by the judge or justice of a court of record of the county or district in which the alleged lunatic resides; and said judge or justice may institute inquiry and take proofs as to any alleged lunacy, before approving or disapproving of such certificate, and may, in his discretion, call a jury in each case to determine the question of lunacy.

Section 2 required that "the examining physicians be of reputable character, graduates of some incorporated medical college, permanent residents of the state and engaged in the actual practice of their profession for at least three years," and such qualifications had to be certified to by a judge of a court of record. Section 3 prohibited any physicians from certifying to the insanity of any person for the purpose of

[1] *Laws* of 1874, chap. 446.

[2] *Ibid.*

[3] Report on a codification of the Laws relating to the Insane, with proposed amendments thereto, *Senate Doc.* 86, Session 1874.

committing him to an asylum of which the said physician was either superintendent, proprietor, an officer, or a regular professional attendant therein.

Previously, county judges or superintendents of the poor had committed patients without the certificates of physicians, and up to this time legislation had been considered chiefly with a view to protecting the public against dangerous persons.

In order that the Commissioner in Lunacy might have proper assistance when making any investigation into the general management and administration of any asylum, public or private, in which insane persons were detained, a law was passed in 1878,[1] providing that " whenever he shall undertake any such investigation, he shall give due notice thereof to the district attorney of the county in which the institution is located, and that it shall be the duty of such district attorney to appear at such investigation in behalf of the people."

On May 13, 1879, a law was passed abolishing the New York State Inebriate Asylum and converting it into the Binghamton Asylum for the Chronic Insane.[2] The latter was opened for the reception of patients of the chronic pauper class from poor-houses in October, 1881. There was no further legislation of importance until 1887 [3] when the St. Lawrence State Asylum at Ogdensburg was established. This institution was opened to receive patients in 1890.

III. COUNTY CARE OF INSANE

There were at this time seven state and three county asylums for the insane.[4] Despite this fact, the number of

[1] *Laws* of 1878, chap. 47, sec. 2.

[2] *Laws* of 1879, chap. 280.

[3] *Laws* of 1887, chap. 375.

[4] State Commissioner in Lunacy, *Annual Report*, 1888, p. 99.

insane in almshouses was still as great as in 1869, when the Willard Asylum was opened. The growth of the general population of the state, which in 1890 reached almost 6,000,000,[1] was so great that the state institutions were inadequate to meet the demands made upon them. In the meantime the movement on the part of the county authorities, which had begun in 1871,[2] for exemption from sending chronic cases to the state institutions, was gradually extended until in 1887 there were 19 counties legally authorized to maintain this class of dependents. A further indication of the pressure brought to bear to bring about the extension of the system of county care of the insane, was the Act passed in 1888 providing for the support, control and management of the chronic insane in Erie County, through the establishment of a county institution.[3]

However, objections to the county system were numerous and of great weight. Its greatest fault was the fact that there was no uniformity in the care bestowed upon patients, nor was there any standard of care. Each county asylum was managed by local men, generally without experience or adequate training and with only a limited knowledge of the requirements of such an institution. The asylums were not under the control of medical men and their management was apt to be governed by considerations of economy rather than of humanity. In consequence of these conditions, as many systems of management were evolved as there were

[1] U. S. Census.

[2] *Laws* of 1871, chap. 713, entitled *An Act in relation to the chronic pauper insane,* authorizing the State Board of Charities to exempt counties from the operation of section 10 of the Willard Asylum Act, which required that all the chronic pauper insane from the poor-houses, and all those discharged not recovered from the State Lunatic Asylum, should be sent to the Willard Asylum (*Laws* of 1865, chap. 342).

[3] *Laws* of 1888, chap. 360.

counties, and the insane thus sheltered failed to get uniform care or adequate and proper treatment.[1]

The true state of affairs at this time (1888) may be surmised from the figures quoted below, from which it will be seen that the number of insane patients outside of state institutions was almost twice as large as within such institutions.[2]

The distribution of insane patients was as follows:

	Number	
State asylums for the acute insane	1,808	
State asylums for the chronic insane	2,851	
State asylums for insane criminals	216	
State asylum for insane emigrants	42	
		4,917

County asylums for acute and chronic insane, viz:

New York	4,439	
Kings	1,531	
Monroe	276	
County asylums for chronic insane	1,763	
Poor-houses	482	
City alms-houses	25	
Private asylums	794	
		9,310
Total		14,227

IV. STATE CARE (*1889-1920*)

The deplorable conditions under which many of the insane in the state had to exist were becoming worse from year to year, due largely to the rapid increase in the general population, and the concomitant increase in the insane population. In 1886, realizing that an end to county care of the insane was imperative, especially from the humanitarian point of

[1] Hurd, *Institutional Care of the Insane*, vol. i, p. 145.

[2] State Commissioner in Lunacy, *Annual Report*, 1888, p. 98.

view, the committee on the insane of the State Charities Aid Association was directed by a resolution of the board of managers, to report, in the form of a bill, a practical plan for removing the dependent insane from the county asylums and poor-houses and placing them under the care of the state.[1]

The State Medical Society joined the State Charities Aid Association in the campaign for legislation to obliterate county care entirely and succeeded in 1889 in obtaining as a preliminary step, the passage of a law creating a new State Commission in Lunacy of three members: a physician, a lawyer and a reputable citizen, the medical member being designated the president of the commission.[2] The following year these same organizations, aided by the new commissioners, were instrumental in getting the State Care Act passed in the face of much opposition from supervisors and superintendents of the poor of exempted counties. This act was based upon a plan drawn up in 1875 by the State Charities Aid Association.[3] The final bill, drafted by a member of the State Charities Aid Association,[4] passed the legislature without amendment, and came to be known as the State Care Act of 1890.[5] This law embodied much con-

[1] State Commissioner in Lunacy, *Annual Report*, 1893, pp. 490-491.

[2] *Laws* of 1889, chap. 283.

[3] State Charities Aid Assn., *Annual Report*, 1875. Dr. C. R. Agnew, Chairman of the Committee on Hospitals, drew up the plan.

[4] Prof. Theodore W. Dwight, Dean of the Columbia College Law School, member of the committee on the insane of the State Charities Aid Assn.

[5] Laws of 1890, chap. 126, entitled *An Act to promote the care and curative treatment of the pauper and indigent insane in the counties of this state, except New York, Kings and Monroe counties, and to permit said excepted counties or either of them, in accordance with the action of their respective local authorities, to avail themselves or anyone of them, of the provisions of this act.*

tained in the law creating the State Commissioner in Lunacy,[1] but eradicated completely county care, except in the case of New York, Kings and Monroe Counties, where the asylums became state institutions within the following six years.[2] The existing state asylums were enlarged as rapidly as possible [3] in order to provide accommodations for about 2,200 additional patients,[4] all of whom were transferred to state care in the course of two or three years.

Under the provisions of the State Care Act,[5] the state was divided into as many asylum districts as there were state insane asylums in the state, and provision was made to either change or increase the districts as necessity demanded. As a result of the early experiences with the office of State Commissioner in Lunacy, the new law gave the Commission in Lunacy adequate powers, and charged the commission with the execution of the provisions of the State Care Act, conferring on it the power to make such rulings concerning the management of the several institutions as in its judgment seemed desirable and necessary.

The Commission in Lunacy was formally organized in June, 1889, and at once set about the performance of the duties assigned. The first inspection by the commissioners of all county asylums and poor-houses of the state convinced them that exclusive state care was absolutely necessary, and the presentation of a report to the legislature on conditions as found by them did much to hasten the full establishment

[1] *Laws* of 1874, chap. 446.

[2] *Laws* of 1891, chap. 335, entitled *An Act for the conversion of Monroe County Insane Asylum into a state hospital, as provided in Section 14, Chapter 126, Laws of 1890.*

[3] Appropriations for this purpose were made to the various state hospitals by *Laws* of 1891, chap. 91.

[4] State Commission in Lunacy, *Annual Report*, 1893, pp. 5-6.

[5] *Laws* of 1890, chap. 126, sec. 1.

of state care.[1] The commission, even before the enactment of the State Care Act, had been granted powers more extensive in their scope and of greater authority than those enjoyed by the British Commission at that time.[2] Among the immediate results of the Acts of 1889 and 1890 was one that was not at first contemplated, namely, the removal to state hospitals by certain non-exempted counties, of the so-called chronic insane who had been kept in custody in the county poor-houses in clear violation of the law. Thus within one year 23 counties were entirely relieved of their insane;[3] in 1894 Queens County abandoned its suit against the state in resistance to the requirements of the State Care Act, and all its insane remaining patients in the wretched institution at Mineola were transferred to the Hudson River State Hospital at Poughkeepsie.[4]

It should be noted that much of the opposition to state care for the insane centered about the division of the insane by law and practice into two classes, the curable and the incurable. The thought was that the insane who were believed to be beyond cure might need less medical attendance, and less of all other comforts and enjoyments which go to make life bearable to this unfortunate class.[5]

By the year 1895 the dependent insane of fifty-nine of the sixty counties of the state were under state care and treatment in state hospitals.[6] Kings County was admitted by an

[1] State Commission in Lunacy, *Annual Report*, 1889, pp. 19-21, 43, 45.

[2] Riggs, C. E., "Progress in the Care of the Insane in the last 20 Years," *N. C. C. C.*, 1893.

[3] State Commission in Lunacy, *Annual Report*, 1890, p. 32.

[4] S. C. in L., *Annual Report*, 1894, p. 5.

[5] S. C. in L., *Annual Report*, 1891, p. 285.

[6] S. C. in L., *Annual Report*, 1895, p. 7.

act of the legislature of this year.[1] The attempt was made in the same year to put New York County under the State Care Act but the bill to convert the New York City Asylums into the Manhattan State Hospitals failed to become a law. The authorities of New York City at this time began to question the constitutionality of the State Care Act, insofar as under its provisions New York County had to pay not only for the care and maintenance of its own insane, but also had to contribute its share of the state tax. It should be noted that the tax had been paid for a period of nearly sixty years.[2] However, the difficulty was solved and state care for all New York State consummated by the enactment of a law in 1896 covering New York County.[3]

The effect of the enactment and practical application of the State Care Act in New York was not only felt throughout the United States[4] but influenced legislation along similar lines in countries in America and in Europe.[5] The energy of those connected with the management of the state hospitals was fully occupied, during the first decade of state care (1890-1900), with the completion of the general frame-work of the system, with bringing the great metropolitan hospitals into it, and with establishing, at least in statutory form, the outlines of a coordinated and organized state system. This accomplished, the next decade was de-

[1] *Laws* of 1895, chap. 628, entitled *An Act for the transfer of the grounds, buildings and equipment of the Kings County Lunatic asylums, with their inmates to the state, and for the establishment in lieu thereof of the Long Island State Hospital.*

[2] New York City Dept. of Public Charities and Corr., *Annual Report,* 1894, p. 58.

[3] *Laws* of 1896, chap. 2, entitled *An Act for the conversion of New York City asylums for the insane into a state hospital, and to establish the Manhattan State Hospital.*

[4] Hurd, *op. cit.*, vol. i, p. 324.

[5] State Com. in Lunacy, *Annual Report,* 1895, p. 7.

voted to developing the smooth and efficient operation of all of the state hospitals under conditions established by the new system. Due to the large number of insane cared for in state hospitals, it has been necessary to develop a system of smooth, efficient, and economical administration. It is the practical application of the State Care Act, as well as in the act itself, that many other states and countries have been interested.[1]

The benefits and achievements resulting from the enactment of the State Care Act in 1890 are not only numerous, but, as noted below, most important for the proper care and treatment of the insane:

Adoption, on July 1, 1890, of a new and improved form of medical certificate in lunacy, designed to facilitate the commitment of insane persons to institutions, and at the same time to provide the liberty of the individual with better safeguards against wrongful intent than had heretofore existed.[2]

Registration in the office of the commission of all qualified medical examiners in lunacy in the state, thus enabling the commission on receipt of a lunacy certificate to determine if the examiners signing the same are legally qualified to perform these services.[3]

Complete registration in the office of the commission of all persons held in custody as insane, whether in public or private institutions.[4]

Adoption of a uniform system of statistical returns for all hospitals and asylums, public and private.[5]

[1] Folks, Homer, *The State Hospitals at the Parting of the Ways*, address at Buffalo, N. Y., Sept. 6, 1912, p. 4.

[2] State Com. in Lunacy, *Annual Report*, 1890, p. 125.

[3] *Ibid.*, p. 124.

[4] *Ibid.*, p. 124.

[5] *Ibid.*, p. 125.

Provision for the transfer of patients from one institution to another, on the order of the commission, whenever for any sufficient reasons this may be deemed desirable.[1]

Regulation providing for the admission of private patients to state hospitals from any part of the state without restriction as to district, at a maximum rate not to exceed $10.00 per week. The rights of the other patients are protected by the provision that there shall be no distinction between public and private patients in regard to the scale of care and accommodations furnished them.[2]

Provision for the paroling of patients who are not regarded as homicidal, suicidal, or otherwise dangerous for a period of six months, during any portion of which they may be returned to the hospital without a new process of commitment. This permits patients whose condition warrants it to go home on trial before final discharge.[3]

Change in the legal title of the state institutions from asylum to hospital.[4]

Division of state into districts dependent upon number of cases and accommodations.[5]

[1] Recommendation for regulation relating to transfer of patients made by Com. in Lunacy in Annual Report of 1889. State Care Act of 1890 made such provision. See State Com. in Lunacy, *Annual Report*, 1893, pp. 75-76.

[2] State Com. in Lunacy, *Annual Report*, 1890, p. 30. State Care Act only contemplated the public or indigent insane. All pay patients were absolutely excluded from its consideration. This necessitated the issuance of the regulation. See State Com. in Lunacy, *Annual Report*, 1890, p. 82.

[3] State Com. in Lunacy, *Annual Report*, 1890, p. 163. Recommendation first made that a law be enacted permitting patients to be disdischarged on parole.

Laws of 1917, chap. 335, extended parole period to not exceeding one year.

[4] State Com. in Lunacy, *Annual Report*, 1890, pp. 15-16.

[5] *Ibid.*, p. 25.

Provision requiring relatives who are legally liable to do so to pay at the rate of $10.00 per week or less.[1]

Abolition of spoils system in appointing medical officers through adoption of plan of civil service examinations.[2]

Maintenance of a training school for nurses made obligatory by amendment to law in 1895.[3]

Creation of a psychiatric institute at Ward's Island, with special courses of instruction for benefit of medical officers at the various hospitals.[4]

Appointment of a medical inspector to visit and inspect the state hospitals and other institutions for the insane, and to examine all patients admitted, subject to the direction of the commission. All the state and private institutions are under the general supervision of the commission.[5]

Abolition of mechanical restraint and substitution of prolonged baths and occasional seclusion for brief periods in treatment of violent and disturbed patients.[6]

Segregation and special treatment of tuberculous insane.[7]

Establishment of a system of after-care of the insane in collaboration with the State Charities Aid Association.[8] At the present time this work is carried on practically independently of the association by the State Hospital Commission.

Establishment of a bureau of deportation, to return to other states and countries deportable cases.[9]

[1] *Laws* of 1896, chap. 545, sec. 69; *Laws* of 1910, chap. 389, sec. 85.

[2] State Com. in Lunacy, *Annual Report*, 1890, pp. 93-94,

[3] *Ibid.*, 1896, pp. 124-125.

[4] State Com. in Lunacy, *Annual Report*, 1895, p. 104; *Annual Report*, 1896, pp. 75-79.

[5] *Ibid.*

[6] State Com. in Lunacy, *Annual Report*, 1901, p. 35.

[7] *Ibid.*

[8] State Hospital Com. *Annual Report*, 1916, p. 121.

[9] *Laws* of 1912, chap. 121, sec. 19.

Change in the name of the State Lunacy Commission to the State Hospital Commission.[1]

Promotion of the work of the State Charities Aid Association in opening clinics for nervous and mental diseases in the large centers, in cooperation with the medical staffs of the nearest hospitals.[2] Though the original impetus to after-care and preventive work in this state came from the State Charities Aid Association, it never established any clinics of its own, except in the sense that the association urged their establishment and took some part in the physical arrangement thereof, as well as in the provision of social service workers. In the establishment and operation of the out-patient departments of the various state hospitals, the rôle of the association has been merely that of an interested, cooperating outsider.

V. RECEPTION OR PSYCHOPATHIC HOSPITALS

Between the years 1880 and 1890, medical men began to realize that in order to increase the ratio of recoveries among insane persons, radical changes would have to be made in the methods of treatment, especially insofar as acute cases were concerned. Dr. Frederick Peterson, subsequently Commissioner of Lunacy in New York, especially urged the desirability of the erection of psychopathic hospitals arranged for the treatment of acute mental cases.[3] In 1888 the Commissioner in Lunacy reviewed the work of the pavilion for the insane in Bellevue Hospital, New York City, and found that one-fourth of the persons admitted at that time were discharged as not insane, as they were, for the most part, persons addicted to the excessive use of intoxicating liquors or drugs.[4] This pavilion, however, now

[1] *Laws* of 1912, chap. 121, sec. 2.

[2] State Hospital Com. *Annual Report*, 1916, pp. 121-122.

[3] Hurd, *op. cit.*, vol. i, p. 258.

[4] State Commissioner in Lunacy, *Annual Report*, 1888, p. 188.

as in 1888, receives patients for observation only, in order to determine whether or not they should be sent to a state hospital.

The movement for the establishment of reception hospitals and pavilions throughout the state continued, and in 1891 the State Commission in Lunacy, in its report to the legislature, recommended "that the Legislature require counties (except New York) to provide suitable places of detention for persons pending examination as to their insanity, to be known as receiving pavilions."[1] No action was taken at this time nor for some years thereafter.

It was not until 1900 that a definite recommendation for the erection of a reception hospital was made by the State Charities Aid Association.[2] The plan advocated provided for the accommodation of 600 patients by the erection, in several of the largest cities of the state, of comparatively small reception or psychopathic hospitals as branches of the existing state hospitals. These new institutions were to be designed for the reception and temporary treatment of insane patients. The reception hospital for New York City was to be a branch of the Manhattan State Hospital and take the place of the wards for the insane at Bellevue. Furthermore, the thought was that these newer and better equipped institutions should be prepared to care for (1) excited cases, (2) restless and suicidal cases, (3) quiet cases, (4) private or paying patients.[3] The State Commission in Lunacy estimated in 1901 that such a hospital on Manhattan Island should accommodate from 100 to 200

[1] State Com. in Lunacy, *Annual Report*, 1891, p. 529.

[2] State Com. in Lunacy, *Annual Report*, 1900; Report of State Charities Aid Association, p. 1054.

[3] Peterson, Frederick, "New Paths is Psychiatry," *Phila. Medical Journal*, June 11, 1898; "A Visit to the Newest Psychopathic Hospital," *Medical News*, Jan. 20, 1900; "Some of the Problems of the Alienist," *American Journal of Ins.*, vol. lvi, no. 1, 1899.

patients, and a similar one in Brooklyn from 50 to 100 patients.[1] It is quite obvious that because of the large increase in the population of Greater New York and the state as a whole, these estimates would now be too low.

Reception hospitals in the United States have been in operation for a number of years in Boston, Baltimore, and Ann Arbor, as well as in Albany, as a part of the general hospital.[2] For smaller cities and towns, these reception or psychopathic hospitals may properly become wards of a general hospital. In a large city like New York, however, with its hundreds of admissions to state hospitals every year, a special institution would have to be created.

It is self-evident that the mentally sick should be permitted the same rights of treatment for their various illnesses as the physically sick, that they should be accorded the same consideration, and that the hospitals of the several cities should be prepared to receive, care for, and intelligently treat them. This means that somewhere in a city there should be wards specially designed and maintained for the receipt, care and treatment, of patients suffering from mental diseases.[3] Such wards or hospitals, adequately equipped and properly officered, with organic connections with a large municipal or state hospital, would be the centers where all persons ailing mentally would receive prompt and effective advice and treatment,[4] and from which would radiate all efforts at popular instruction in matters

[1] State Com. in Lunacy, *Annual Report*, 1901, p. 31.

[2] Hurd, *op. cit.*, vol. i, pp. 258, 259.

[3] For results of treatment in psychopathic hospital, see "Analysis of Recoveries at the Psychopathic Hospital, Boston," by Thomas H. Haines, in *Boston Medical and Surgical Journal*, Dec. 31, 1914. Also similar study by E. E. Southard, M.D., *Boston Medical and Surgical Journal*, Sept. 24, 1914.

[4] White, William A., "Dividing Line between General Hospital and Hospital for the Insane," *The Modern Hospital*, March 1914; State Com. in Lunacy, *Annual Report*, 1902, pp. 83-84.

connnected with mental disease. A psychopathic hospital or department, in conjunction with its other functions, should serve as a prophylactic and educational station. Standing in a community on the plane with the general hospital, or other specialized hospital, it emphasizes mental disease as a disease, and should serve as a center to which may come for advice and counsel, those suffering from psychoneuroses and the early stages of mental disease, as easily and freely as they would seek out a general hospital in case of organic illness.[1]

The State Commission in Lunacy, as well as the State Charities Aid Association, both strongly advocated for a number of years the construction of a series of psychopathic hospitals throughout the state for the reception and treatment of acute curable cases.[2] In 1902 a law was passed providing that accommodations be obtained or provided for the observation and treatment of a limited number of insane persons.[3] A year later a bill to establish a reception hospital for the insane was introduced in the legislature but failed to pass.[4] The following year (1904) the same bill was introduced and was passed with slight modification.[5]

[1] Williams, Frankwood E., "Psychopathic Hospitals and Prophylaxis," *Boston Medical and Surgical Journal*, June 24, 1915, pp. 933, 935.

[2] State Com. in Lunacy, *Annual Report*, 1902, pp. 7, 1027-1029.

[3] *Laws* of 1902, chap. 593, providing that "The Commission shall provide accommodations in the City of New York for a hospital to receive a limited number of alleged insane, and insane persons, where skilled observation is necessary in making required pathological and psychopathic research and examination. Admission to the hospital hereby created shall be regulated by the Commission."

[4] State Com. in Lunacy, *Annual Report*, 1903, p. 956.

[5] *Laws* of 1904, chap. 760, entitled *An Act authorizing the City of New York to acquire a site and to lease the same to the state for the establishment thereon of a reception hospital for the insane.* The hospital thus to be erected was to have accommodations for not less than 200 patients, and the sum of Three Hundred Thousand Dollars was to be spent for the erection of the necessary buildings.

In 1905 an appropriation of $150,000 was made by the legislature toward the erection of the hospital,[1] and action was taken to obtain cooperation between the State Commission in Lunacy and the New York City authorities.[2] A site for the proposed psychopathic or reception hospital was finally acquired by the City of New York, but upon investigation by the Commission in Lunacy it was found that the site was unsuited for the purpose intended for a number of reasons, among them the inaccessibility of the plot, its meagre extent, and its noisy neighbors.[3]

The State Hospital Commission[4] passed a resolution in 1912 referring the consideration of the question of the pyschopathic hospital and the site selected by the city, to a committee consisting of the superintendents of four state hospitals in the metropolitan district and three other members.[5] At a meeting held July 24, 1912, a decision was reached to the effect that " it was the sense of this committee that the time is not yet ripe for the establishment of an insitution such as proposed, and that therefore, the city be notified that the state is at present unable to proceed with

[1] State Com. in Lunacy, *Annual Report*, 1905, p. 27.

[2] *Ibid.*, pp. 1093-1094.

[3] State Com. in Lunacy, *Annual Report*, 1908, pp. 65-66. The site was situated between 73d and 74th streets, near the East River, a neighborhood far from being suited for the purpose of a psychopathic hospital.

[4] Name of State Commission in Lunacy changed to State Hospital Commission by *Laws* of 1912, chap. 121, sec. 2.

[5] The full committee was composed of Dr. August Hoch, director of the Psychiatric Institute, Wards Island; Dr. William Mabon, Supt. of Manhattan State Hospital; Dr. G. A. Smith, Supt. of Central Islip State Hospital; Dr. Wm. A. Macey, Supt. of Kings Park State Hospital; Dr. E. M. Somers, Supt. of Long Island State Hospital, and Mr. Homer Folks of the State Charities Aid Association. (*Vide Annual Report*, State Hospital Com., 1912, p. 84.)

the erection of a reception hospital." [1] After further consideration of the entire project by the commission, it was concluded that such an undertaking would not be justifiable at the time, owing to the large expenditures necessary for the maintenance of the department as a whole.[2] Legislaion was enacted in 1913 for the purpose of authorizing the commission, on behalf of the state, to surrender to the City of New York the indenture of lease for the property lying between 73d and 74th streets and the East River.[3] Thus ended, for the time being, the attempt to secure a psychopathic hospital for New York City. It should be noted that the principle of the necessity of such hospitals was sustained, but that, due to the existing overcrowding in the metropolitan district hospitals, relief in this direction was considered of paramount importance, as inexpensive additions to the then existing establishments were thought necessary to bring about an alleviation of the overcrowding. And indeed, the hospitals continue to be overcrowded,[4] in spite of the fact that additions to the existing institutions have been built. Whether or not the State Commission was right in reversing its policy of insisting upon the erection of a psychopathic hospital for New York City may become more evident from what follows. Be that as it may, an institution for the insane or mentally ill, in which all disturbing and distressing features, all confusing and fatiguing agencies will be prohibited, is essential for the cure and

[1] The only dissenting member was Mr. Homer Folks, who was of opinion that a hospital should be built (24th A. R., S. H. C., p. 85).

[2] State Hospital Com., *Annual Report*, 1912-1913, p. 62.

[3] *Laws* of 1913, chap. 678.

[4] On June 30, 1918, the 13 civil hospitals, with a capacity of 28,997, housed 35,462 patients, an overcrowding of 6,465 patients, or 22.3 per cent. The overcrowding has been around the 6,000 mark for a number of years. (35th A. R., S. H. C., 1917-1918, p. 235.)

relief of the mentally sick. Recoveries of acute mental cases depend to a great extent upon the nature of the initial care. Such care, as described above, can be given in a psychopathic hospital; and the agitation for these institutions will continue until efforts in this direction are crowned with success.

VI. HOSPITAL DEVELOPMENT COMMISSION

The urgent necessity for relief of the overcrowded conditions existing in the state hospitals prior to 1914, and since aggravated by the war,[1] became apparent to the legislature in 1917, when Chapter 238 was passed. This law created the Hospital Development Commission and authorized large expenditures for new buildings.[2] The measure in brief provides for a survey of the state hospitals for the insane, the development and adoption of a plan to provide for the present surplus and the future increase in the patients, and directs the commission to recommend to the legislature each year the appropriation necessary to complete one-tenth of the entire hospital development plan. The measure also provides for the investigation of the problem of the care of the feeble-minded and the development of a plan for its solution.[3]

[1] During the year 1916-1917 only 27 patients were deported, less than 7 per cent of the number deported under normal conditions. (29th A. R., S. H. C., p. 166.) During the year 1917-1918 the total number of aliens deported was 53, as compared with 825 in 1914. (30th A. R., S. H. C., p. 77.)

[2] Hospital Development Commission to consist of State Engineer, Chairman of State Hospital Commission, State Architect, Chairman Senate Finance Commission, Chairman Assembly Ways and Means Committee, two members to be appointed by Governor, one member of Legislature, who shall be a minority member of one of the financial committees of Legislature, to be named by Minority leaders of Senate and Assembly.

[3] 29th A. R., S. H. C., pp. 50-51.

Shortly after the organization of the commission,[1] the State Charities Aid Association brought to the attention of the members of the new body the fact that the establishment of psychopathic hospitals is an important part of any complete program for the care and cure of the insane.[2] In its report to the legislature of February 18, 1918, the Hospital Development Commission recommended the establishment of a psychiatric hospital on Manhattan Island, and gave its reasons for this action, outlining very briefly the nature and purposes of such an institution.[3] After the submission of this report the Committee on Metropolitan District of the Comission continued its visits and studies of all the existing psychopathic hospitals in the United States. These continued investigations strengthened the committee's conviction that a psychopathic hospital was urgently needed on Manhattan Island as part of the state hospital system. The committee prepared a report detailing plans which, in its judgment, should be followed in organizing such an institution.

The purposes of the institution should be:[4]

(A) *Treatment*—To reach persons suffering from mental disorders in their early and often curable stages, and lead them back to mental health without the sup-

[1] In the constitutional convention held in 1915 the proposal was made that a 20-year program be provided for the development of the state hospitals, in order to remove these institutions from the field of politics. (N. Y. Constitutional Convention, 1915, *Revised Record*, pp. 2883-2885.)

[2] Memorandum submitted to the Hospital Development Commission by the Committee on Mental Hygiene of the State Charities Aid Association, November 1917. This contained a concise and forceful statement of the problem and ways of meeting it, *etc.*

[3] *N. Y. State Hospital Quarterly*, August 1918; *Mental Hygiene*, Jan. 1919, p. 113.

[4] 30th A. R., S. H. C., 1917-1918, pp. 67-71.

posed stigma of legal commitment to an asylum for the insane. Entrance to be made easy. Many cases would thus be saved from prolonged stays in a state hospital.

(B) *Research*—To develop, through study and research, more and more methods, by which mental maladies may be prevented or recognized in their early stages, and by which they may be successfully treated.

(C) *Teaching*—To endeavor to spread abroad a better knowledge and understanding of mental disorders, with a view of securing effective cooperation in coping with them

(D) *Service to State Hospitals*—To serve as a place where each new plan of treatment that is seriously proposed shall be studied and tried out, with a view to its introduction, if found worthy, into the other institutions of the system

Legislation seems to have assured the eventual establishment of a state psychopathic hospital in New York City, long advocated as an urgent need to round out the system of state care of the insane. The chief results that may be hoped for as a result of this legislation are as follows:

(A) Such hospitals will help check the present rapid increase in the number of insane by heading off the stream at its source.

(B) Such hospitals, by preventing and curing cases of mental disease in incipient and early stages, will prevent their becoming chronic insane patients, and will save the state the expense of continuous care of chronic cases for a long term of years in regular state hospitals.

(C) These hospitals, by receiving and caring for recent

and acute cases of insanity, will diminish the numbers annually committed to the other state hospitals, and so will relieve the overcrowding in these hospitals.

An expenditure of $700,000 was authorized by the legislature in 1920 for the construction of buildings and the development of the grounds of the new psychopathic hospital.[1] Plans have already been drawn by the state architect for a state psychopathic hospital in New York City, for which it is hoped the city will be persuaded to provide a site. These plans have been considered by the Hospital Development Commission and are now being studied by the commission's medical committee and other medical experts. If they are approved by the commission, it is likely that an effort will be made to hasten the erection of this most important adjunct of the state hospital system.

In the foregoing pages the attempt has been made to present an outline of the most important phases of legislation affecting the insane in New York State, and to lay the background and prepare the field for a further consideration of the problems involved in dealing with this group of the state's charges. The following chapters will consider a large number of cases of insanity as at present handled, and will indicate the social implications of the problem as a whole.

[1] *Laws* of 1920, chap. 860.

CHAPTER II

Insanity as a Community Problem

I. CASES STUDIED

THE cosmopolitan nature of the population of New York City makes it the most fertile field of study for the group of cases under consideration. Material for both social and clinical observation is found here in abundance, and it is because of these facts that this study is limited to a particular group of cases, namely, the Jewish patients admitted to the psychopathic or observation wards, male and female, of Bellevue Hospital during a twelve-month period. The writer has had unusual opportunities to observe and work with Jewish psychopathic cases for several years and it is his hope that out of such studies and observations as he and others in this field may be able to make and record, methods in the social care of the insane may be formulated and made the basis of further studies, as well as used as guides in the social care of the insane, irrespective of race or nationality.

II. INCIDENCE OF INSANITY AMONG JEWS

(a) *In European Countries.* For years it has been maintained by the psychiatrical world that the Jewish race contributed more cases of insanity than any other race.[1] Of late years, however, some investigators in this field have

[1] Brill, A. A. and Karpas, M. J., "Insanity among Jews," *Medical Record,* Oct. 3, 1914, pp. 576-578.

begun to doubt this traditional view; they have found that it was not sufficiently demonstrated that the Jew differed in his liability to insanity from the Gentile, and some have gone so far as to assert that the converse is true.[1] This conclusion was also reached a few years ago by the United States Department of Commerce which stated in its report: "On the contrary, facts from which deductions can be made point rather to a comparatively smaller amount of insanity among Jews than among people of several other races."[2] Studies of the incidence of insanity among Jews have been made in a number of European countries where these people have lived for many centuries. Lombroso found that the seemingly larger percentage of insanity among Jews was not so much a matter of race as of intellectual work, for among the Semitic races in general (Arabs, Bedouins) insanity is very rare.[3] The results of a more recent study of the problem as it exists in Germany were published in 1909 by Sichel, whose deductions were based on careful investigations of the records of the Frankfort Hospital for the insane. He found that although there were relatively more Jewish inmates than the corresponding percentage of the Jewish population in Frankfort, this could only be demonstrated in reference to certain groups of mental disorders; however, the other types revealed a smaller percentage of Jews than of non-Jews.[4] Studies by A. Pilcz in Vienna and C. F. Beadles in London seem to indicate a higher percentage of insanity among Jews than

[1] Brill, A. A., "Adjustment of the Jew to the American Environment," *Mental Hygiene*, April, 1918, pp. 219-220.

[2] U. S. Dept. of Commerce Report, quoted in *Mental Hygiene*, April 1918, p. 219.

[3] Lombroso, E., *Crime, Its Causes and Remedies*, 1909, p. 39.

[4] Sichel, Max, *Die Geistesstorungen bei den Juden* (Leipzig, 1909), pp. 43-81.

among non-Jews.[1] In this country Spitzka, in 1880, came to the conclusion after a careful study of the problem, that on the whole the different forms of insanity occur in nearly the same proportions in the Anglo-Saxon, Teutonic, Celtic and Hebrew races.[2] In considering the figures for Europe it should be remembered that in a number of the larger European countries as late as the nineteenth, and in some even in the present century, Jews have been harassed and forced to endure unusual stresses and strains and even the torture of violent death at the hands of their persecutors. For these reasons it would hardly be advisable for the purposes of scientific knowledge and accuracy to consider statistics gathered in such lands. The largest number of Jews within modern times congregated in a limited area are to be found in New York State and City; for this reason the admissions to the psychopathic wards of Bellevue Hospital, New York City, have been made the basis of the statistical study of the problem considered in this work.

(b) *Insanity in Rural and Urban Districts.* The total number of first admissions to the civil state hospitals in New York for 1917 was as follows: males 3,605; females 3,272; total 6,877. Of these 398 males and 402 females, a total of 800, were Jewish, or 11.0 per cent males and 12.3 per cent females, with a general average of 11.6 per cent.[3] The total state population in 1917 was 9,917,438,[4] the total Jewish population was approximately 1,600,000,[5] or 16.0

[1] *Jewish Encyclopedia,* article "Insanity," vol. vi, p. 606.

[2] Spitzka, Edward C., "Race and Insanity," *Journal for Nervous and Mental Diseases,* 1880.

[3] State Hospital Commission, 29th Annual Report, 1916-1917, p. 426.

[4] S. H. C., 30th A. R., 1917-1918, p. 57.

[5] *Jewish Communal Register,* New York City, 1917, p. 89; Dushkin, Alexander M., *A Survey of Jewish Religious Education in New York City,* (Dissertation Teacher's College, Columbia Univ., 1918) in which

per cent of the general population. In 1918 the figures were about the same—total number of first admissions, 6,797; total number of Jewish patients, first admissions, 832.[1] The figures indicate a much lower percentage of insanity among Jews in the state than in the remaining general population. It should be observed also that very close to 100 per cent of the Jews in the state live in New York City, only a small proportion living in the other cities in the state, with very few in the rural districts.

During the year 1910 the urban population of the United States contributed 102.8 admissions and the rural but 41.4 admissions per 100,000 of the population to the institutions for the insane and feebleminded.[2] An important factor having a bearing upon this question is the difference between the two portions of the population in age distribution; only 27.2 per cent of the urban population and as many as 36.3 per cent of the rural population falls in the group under 15 years of age, a group contributing but a small fraction of the admissions to institutions for the insane.[3] The marked difference between urban and rural commitments, especially in New York State, is still further emphasized by the fact that the rate of first admissions per 100,000 population is much higher in the counties of the state in which cities are located than in those in which there are few, if any, cities of considerable size. Thus, the rate per 100,000 population for New York County in 1918 was 105.9, whereas it was

the Jewish population for New York City in 1917 is placed at 1,500,000. Chalmers, Henry, "Jews in New York City," *Amer. Jour. of Statistics*, 1914-1915, placed the Jewish population at 1,330,000 in 1913, pp. 68-75. *American Jewish Year Book*, 1919-1920, p. 605, estimates the Jewish population in New York State in 1918 as 1,603,923.

[1] S. H. C., 30th A. R., 1917-1918, p. 405.

Insane and Feebleminded in Institutions, Bureau of Census, 1914, p. 27.

[3] De Fursac, R. and Rosanoff, A., *Manual of Psychiatry*, 1916, p. 15.

only 29.9 in Warren County, 30.7 in Schoharie County, *etc.*[1] As aforementioned, the Jewish first admissions to the civil state hospitals in 1917 and 1918 averaged about 11.6 per cent of the total first admissions, while they formed approximately 16.0 per cent of the general population of the state, indicating a rather low rate of first admissions to institutions for the insane.

(c) *Jewish Insane in New York City.* Another definite and perhaps somewhat more exact way to arrive at the ratio of the occurrence of insanity among Jews to their proportion in the general population is to consider the admissions to the psychopathic wards of Bellevue Hospital, New York City, for there the population is practically all urban, the admissions are all from the city proper (nearly altogether from the Boroughs of Manhattan and the Bronx), and the Jewish population is centered in the city.

The number of admissions to the psychopathic wards, male and female, of Bellevue Hospital from September 1, 1917 to August 31, 1918, totalled 6,878, of which 1,127 or 16.38 per cent were Jews. For the following year, beginning September 1, 1918 and ending August 31, 1919, the total number of admissions to the psychopathic wards of Bellevue Hospital was 8,255, of which 1,133 or 13.72 per cent were Jews. During the second year, as has been noted, the total number of admissions was considerably larger than the year previous. This can be accounted for by stating that directly after the signing of the armistice on November 11, 1918, the number of cases of alcoholism and alchoholic psychoses admitted to the psychopathic wards increased considerably; also, during this year a number of soldiers who had become insane while in service in various camps in the United States were sent to Bellevue Hospital,

[1] S. H. C., 30th A. R., 1917-1918, p. 438.

psychopathic division, and later transferred to their relatives in the city. The incidence of alcoholism and alcoholic psychoses among Jews, as will be pointed out later, has been considerably less than in almost any other element of the general population of New York, and for this reason, using the Bellevue Hospital figures, the percentage of insanity among Jews was 13.72 per cent for 1918-1919; whereas it had reached 16.38 per cent the year previous. The total population of New York City in 1917 was approximately 5,800,000;[1] the total Jewish population about 1,500,000, or 25.8 per cent of the general population, with admission rates to the psychopathic wards of Bellevue Hispital of 16.38 per cent one year and 13.72 per cent the following year.

To Bellevue Hospital are brought the insane or alleged insane from the Boroughs of Manhattan and the Bronx only. Kings County Hospital in Brooklyn receives such patients from the Boroughs of Kings and Queens; Richmond Borough, with a Jewish population of only 5,000, sends its insane directly to Manhattan State Hospital after examination by two local physicians. A consideration of the total admissions to the psychopathic wards of both Bellevue and Kings County Hospitals for two years, thus including practically the entire city, will give a still better and more accurate index of the occurrence of insanity among the Jews of New York. The total number of admissions to Kings County Hospital, psychopathic wards, from September 1, 1917 to August 31, 1918 was 2,326, of which 392 or 16.85 per cent were Jews. For the following year, September 1, 1918 to August 31, 1919 the total admissions were 2,550, of which 429 or 16.82 per cent were Jews, there being in both years a markedly lower rate of

[1] Dept. of Health, New York City, estimated the total population on July 1, 1917, at 5,737,492, *Weekly Bulletin*, July 7, 1917, p. 223.

admissions than the percentage of the total population. For the entire city (exclusive of Richmond, which is practically negligible) Table I indicates the admissions and percentages:

TABLE I. TOTAL ADMISSIONS TO THE PSYCHOPATHIC WARDS, NEW YORK CITY

Year.	Bellevue Hospital.		Kings Co. Hospital.		Total in City.	Total Jew. in City.	Per cent Jew. in City.
	Total.	Jew.	Total.	Jew.			
1917–18	6,878	1,127	2,326	392	9,204	1,519	16.50
1918–19	8,255	1,133	2,550	429	10,805	1,562	14.45

In view of what has been said regarding the unusually large total admissions to Bellevue Hospital for the year 1918-1919, it might be advisable to make sufficient allowance for the increase over the preceding year by setting the total admissions at about what they were in 1917-1918. In any event, the percentage of Jewish admissions for the entire city would not average over 16.5 per cent, which is considerably less than 25.8 per cent, the proportion of Jews in the general population of New York City.

III. METHODS OF COMMITTING PATIENTS TO STATE HOSPITALS

(a) *Legal Provisions for Commitment.* The patients admitted to the psychopathic wards of Bellevue Hospital came from various sources, usually being brought there by the special ambulance attached to the psychopathic service of the hospital. The transference of the patients to the hospital is carried out under authority of Section 87, of Article 4, Chapter 27 of the Consolidated Laws known as the "Insanity Law" relative to the transfer of alleged insane persons to the psychopathic wards of Bellevue Hospital, the law reading as follows:

It shall be the duty of such trustees of Bellevue and Allied Hospitals . . . to see that the proceedings are taken for the determination of the mental condition of any such person in the boroughs or counties mentioned, who comes under their observation or is reported to them as apparently insane, and, when necessary, to see that proceedings are instituted for the commitment of such person to an institution for the care of the insane; provided that such report is made by any person with whom such alleged person may reside, or at whose house he may be, or by the father, mother, husband, wife, brother, sister, or child of any such person, or next of kin available, or by any duly licensed physician, or by any police officer, or by the representative of any incorporated society doing charitable or philanthropic work. When the trustees of Bellevue and Allied Hospitals are thus informed of an apparently insane person, residing in the boroughs of Manhattan or the Bronx . . . it shall be the duty of these authorities . . . to send a nurse or a medical examiner in lunacy attached to the psychopathic ward of their institution, or both, to the place where the alleged insane person resides or is to be found. If, in the judgment of the chief resident alienist of the psychopathic ward or of the medical examiner thus sent, the person is in immediate need of care and treatment or observation for the purpose of ascertaining his mental condition, he shall be removed to the psychopathic ward for a period not to exceed ten days, and the person or persons most nearly related to him, so far as the same can be readily ascertained by such trustees . . . shall be notified of such removal.

This section of the law went into effect March 5, 1912, when the old law was amended. Prior to the amendment, patients were brought to the psychopathic wards by the police as prisoners, or committed for examination by city magistrates. Such procedure greatly aggravated the mental infirmities, which require more tender, skillful and gentle handling than medical and surgical cases. Since this measure has became operative and experienced nurses and a special ambulance are sent for the patients, thus eliminating the police as arresting agents and the court procedures, the number of excited and disturbed patients received in the psychopathic wards has greatly decreased, and straps, handcuffs, and police patrol wagons have been altogether done away with.[1]

The legal right of the hospital authorities to go into a home and forcibly remove a patient against his own will was questioned for a time by those interested in the matter of personal rights. The opinion of the Corporation Counsel of the City of New York regarding the interpretation of this section is appended.[2]

The obvious purpose of Section 87 is to sanction and permit the summary removal to the hospitals of alleged insane persons who, by their actions, evince symptoms of insanity, or whose conduct, in the judgment of the medical examiner sent pursuant to its provisions, is such that it would be dangerous to themselves or to the community to allow them to remain unrestrained or would disturb the public peace, and to afford alleged insane persons, in whose cases these elements of danger or disorder are lacking, opportunity to be heard before depriving them of their liberty.

In this view I am of the opinion and advise that it is not contemplated or required by Section 87 that a person alleged to be insane should be forcibly brought to the hospital, unless such person has acted in a disorderly manner, has committed an overt act, or is apparently an immediate source of danger to himself or to the community, and that in other cases,

[1] Bellevue and Allied Hospitals, New York City, A. R., 1912, pp. 68-69.

[2] *Ibid.*, A. R., 1913, p. 64.

recourse should be had to that provision of Section 87 which reads:

"Whenever in the City of New York an information is laid before a magistrate that a person is apparently insane, the magistrate must issue a warrant directed to the sheriff of the county in which the information is made, or any marshal or policeman in the City of New York, reciting the substance of the information and commanding the officer forthwith to arrest the person alleged to be insane and bring him before the magistrate issuing the warrant."

It should be remembered that the procedure of summarily removing a person to the hospital against his will for examination as to his mental condition would seem to deprive the person of his liberty without due process of law, in violation of the fundamental law of the land. However, this section of the statute authorizes this procedure as a police measure, so that whenever there is no element of danger to the individual himself or any danger or disturbance to the community, it would not be within the purport of the law to bring a patient to the hospital in this summary manner. This is particularly applicable to the paranoid types of mental disease, which will be discussed in another part of this chapter.

(b) *Social Workers and Commitment of Patients.* In applying the various provisions of the law, if any difference of opinion exists in the family regarding the mental condition of the patient or his transfer to the hospital for examination, extreme caution must of necessity be exercised in removing him from his residence. When the "request" comes from a physician or a "representative of an incorporated society doing charitable or philanthropic work," without the consent of the family or relatives of the patient, it is usually inadvisable and frequently fraught with harm to remove him summarily from his home.

The ease with which patients may be brought to the hospital might become too great a temptation to social workers and representatives of charitable organizations to hasten patients to the hospital for examination. While in a number of instances such a method is most desirable and beneficial, many neurotic and borderline patients might become greatly upset from the shock incident to such transfer. Every effort should always be made to bring the milder cases of mental trouble to the hospital as voluntary patients, or to take them to mental hygiene clinics in order to ascertain their mental condition and the advisability of transferring them to the hospital for further examination. The intent of this section of the law, empowering representatives of charitable or philanthropic agencies to apply for the mental examination of persons in the psychopathic wards, is altogether a praiseworthy one. However, unless organizations specializing in the care of the mentally sick are specifically called upon, there is, as pointed out above, too much left to the judgment of workers nearly always without training in the observation, care, and understanding of mental cases. Several training schools for social workers have realized this fact and are instituting both theoretical and practical courses for the training of psychiatric social workers.

(c) *The Police and Mental Cases.* As a result of much experience it has been found advisable to have a police officer present at the house of the patient when the ambulance arrives, especially if the patient is unduly excited and liable to do harm to himself or to others if he should see the ambulance and nurses. The presence of a police officer is also at times necessary when the patient has no friends or relatives residing with him; in such instances the duty of the officer is to take care of the personal effects and property of the patient after his removal to the hospital.

On May 5, 1919, an amendment to the insanity law provided that in the City of New York the officer commanded by a warrant to arrest a person alleged to be insane must bring him before the magistrate's court out of which the warrant was issued, instead of before the magistrate issuing the warrant. Though the number of insane or alleged insane persons thus brought to court is small in comparison with the total number committed, still, with the system of rotating magistrates as it exists in New York City, the apparent difficulty and inadvisability of taking an insane person to another section of the city than the one in which he lives, is quite obvious.[1]

One of the difficulties experienced by friends and relatives as well as by mental hygiene workers of private organizations is in having certain patients brought to the hospital without court proceedings. The police department, acting for the Ambulance Board of the city, must be notified when an ambulance is wanted. As a rule a policeman is either asked to telephone for the ambulance or he is at the house when the ambulance calls. The patient, especially if a paranoiac, will speak lucidly and intelligently and the officer frequently accuses the relatives of the patient of attempting to "railroad" the patient to an insane asylum. The same also happens when a hospital interne responds to an ambulance call, and, not having sufficient experience in the diagnosis of mental diseases, refuses to accept the patient for transfer to the hospital. In a number of cases it is for these reasons a matter of weeks before a person whose relatives realize that a condition of mental abnormality exists, is at last brought to the hospital. Once there, the Commitment Law of the state, probably the most practicable in the country, preserves the constitutional rights of the individual. It involves little publicity, is not cumber-

[1] *Laws* of 1919, sec. 87, chap. 380.

some, and is well safeguarded.[1] In other cities in the state the provisions for the care of the insane pending commitment have shown many shortcomings, as such persons have been detained in jails and almshouses. In order to correct this evil a law was passed in 1914 authorizing the State Hospital Commission to enforce its requirements as to suitable care for the dependent insane during the time steps are being completed for their commitment to a state hospital.[2] This has helped reduce the number of instances where improper care is bestowed and within a short time adequate provision for proper care should be found in every county in the state.[3]

There are two methods in which studies of the nature of this work may be made: (1) the statistical method; (2) the case method. It is the purpose to follow both these methods in this study, and it may be well to define the various terms to be used, as well as to present the classification and give a brief definition and review of the different psychoses and neuroses to be considered.

IV. DEFINITION OF TERM "INSANITY"

However, before proceeding to the task of setting forth the definitions spoken of, the question of the meaning or connotation of the concept insanity should be settled if possible.[4] Many attempts have been made to formulate definitions of the term, and several are herein presented for consideration. Thus, White[5] states that insanity is not a

[1] State Comm. in Lunacy, A. R., 1890, p. 125.

[2] *Laws* of 1914, chap. 305. (Incorporated in the Insanity Law as sec. 20.)

[3] S. H. C., 26th A. R., 1913-1914, p. 277.

[4] For a full discussion of the term see article by William A. White on "Underlying Concepts in Mental Hygiene," in *Mental Hygiene*, Jan., 1917, pp. 7-8.

[5] White, William A., *Outlines of Psychiatry*, 1918, p. 17.

disease; it is rather a symbol grouping for a large number of different mental diseases which tend to arrange themselves with greater or less distinctness into circumscribed groups of reaction trends. According to Dercum [1] insanity may be defined as a diseased state in which there is more or less persistent departure from the normal manner of thinking, acting, and feeling. Still another, though kindred interpretation of the term is offered by Craig [2] in stating that a person may be considered of unusual mind if from some mental cause: (1) he is unable to look after himself and his affairs; (2) he is dangerous to himself or to others; (3) he interferes with society, *i. e.*, is unable to adjust himself to his surroundings.[3] Maudsley [4] wrote that the most prominent pathological characteristic of the insane is a complete or almost complete absence of moral feeling and moral ideas. A more concise definition is that offered by Peterson when he states that "insanity is a manifestation in language or conduct of disease or defect of the brain." [5] As a scientific term, *insanity* is falling into disuse and now retains a significance mainly in a legal sense; like lunacy it seems destined to become obsolete.[6] It would be best to restrict the application of the term to cases in which the mental disorder is of such a nature as to render advisable commitment for treatment or custody to a special institution, or care under trained and expert supervision.[7]

[1] Dercum, Francis X., *A Clinical Manual of Mental Disease*, 1914, p. 21.

[2] Craig, Maurice, *Psychological Medicine*, 1905, p. 20.

[3] Mercier, Charles A., *Textbook of Insanity and other Mental Diseases*, 1914, p. 42.

[4] Maudsley, Henry, *Responsibility in Mental Disease*, 1874, pp. 171-172.

[5] Church, A. and Peterson F., *Nervous and Mental Diseases*, 1901, p. 630.

[6] De Fursac and Rosanoff, *op. cit.*, *Introduction*, p. xi.

[7] Peterson, Frederick, *Mental Diseases*, 1899, p. 603, quotes the noted

V. CAUSES OF INSANITY

There has been much speculation as to the causes of insanity, though some factors have been definitely determined upon as being responsible for a large proportion of the cases of mental alienation that fill our state hospitals and cost the various communities and states in the country large sums for their care and treatment.[1] Broadly speaking and with special reference to causation the mental disorders may be divided into two groups: (1) Exogenous, or where the causes are chiefly external; (2) Endogenous, where the existence of external causes or of primary tissue changes in the brain has not been demonstrated. The causes found in this group are internal, the insanity growing, as it were out of the personality.[2] Among causes affecting the first class, are syphilitic infection, poisons introduced into the body, (as alcohol, cocaine, opium and its derivatives, *etc.*) or created within the body, and exhaustion. Heredity plays a most important part in the causation of mental disease in the endogenous group. Kraepelin classifies the causes in this class under the divisions of general predisposition and personal predisposition.[3] Modern physiological psychology

English jurist, Lord Justice Blackburn, who once said while giving evidence before a committee of the House of Commons, "I have read every definition which I could meet with, and never was satisfied with one of them, and have endeavored in vain to make one satisfactory to myself. I verily believe it is not in human power to do so." Clouston, T. S., *Unsoundness of Mind,* 1911, p. 1, also emphasizes the difficulty encountered when attempting to give a satisfactory definition of the term.

[1] Number of patients on books in New York State Hospitals at close of fiscal year June 30, 1918: in civil hospitals 37,352; in hospitals for the criminal insane 1,420. (S. H. C., 30th A. R., 1917-1918, p. 9.) Total expenditures for the year approximately $11,000,000. *Ibid.*, p. 25.

[2] Hoch, August, "The Manageable Causes of Insanity," *New York State Hospitals Bulletin,* Sept., 1909, pp. 1-3. See also Thomson, J. Arthur, *Heredity,* 1908, pp. 263-264, for a discussion of this classification from a somewhat different viewpoint.

[3] Kraepelin, Emil, *Psychiatrie,* Achte Auflage, 1 Band, pp. 140-208.

emphasizes the fact that there are innumerable phenomena which indicate that the mind operates as a true cause within the structure of the body, and that the reverse relation is also true.[1] Considering another method of classification, it may be stated that the essential causes of insanity are heredity, alcoholism, syphilis, and head injuries; and that there are numerous and complex incidental or contributing causes, which in themselves do not suffice to produce insanity, but do so only in the presence of an essential cause. Alcohol and head injuries belong to this class also, as do various psychic conditions, common among which are business and domestic troubles, love affairs, death or illness of relatives. Other etiological factors that may be mentioned are race, age, sex, environment, occupation, marital condition, education, and immigration.[2]

(a) *Heredity*. In any discussion of insanity the question of heredity looms up as probably the most important factor.[3] An inherited predisposition to mental disorder is found in from 30 to 90 per cent of cases according to different authorities.[4] This wide variation in percentages is due to the inability to gather such statistics accurately, the lack of cooperation of relatives in obtaining the necessary information, and the failure to consider large enough groups in such studies to render them of any statistical

[1] Ladd, G. W. and Woodworth, R. S., *Elements of Physiological Psychology*, 1915, pp. 644-646.

[2] De Fursac and Rosanoff, *op. cit.*, pp. 2-20.

[3] Mercier, Charles A., *Crime and Criminals*, 1918, sets forth his doctrine of the causation of insanity, stating that it is due in varying proportions to the two factors of heredity and stress—to the stress of circumstances acting upon an innate constitution; to varying proportions of heredity and environment, p. 225. Mercier, Charles A., *Text-book of Insanity and other Mental Diseases*, 1914, pp. 3-4. For opinions similar to the above see 13th A. R., S. Comm. in Lun., 1900-1901, p. 37.

[4] White, William A., *Outlines of Psychiatry*, 1918, p. 20.

value.[1] In one careful study of a comparatively large number of cases, an investigation by Rosanoff and Orr, the correspondence between the actual findings and the theoretical expectation acording to the Mendelian theory, was very close.[2] However, it is quite apparent that the scientific study of heredity cannot be applied to the diseases of man with as much accuracy as in the vegetable kingdom or among the lower animals. The human race is not open to Mendel's essential methods, and its mere complexity involves innumerable differences from lower forms of life.[3] Among other things, there is general agreement that the appearance or non-appearance of a characteristic may be in part decided by environmental influences.[4] Given the opportunity, certain characters may manifest themselves which without such opportunity must have lain dormant.[5]

Our present-day knowledge of heredity as applied to man is as yet insufficient to permit us to take a definite stand as to the inheritance of psychoses.[6] Furthermore, there is

[1] Church and Peterson, *Mental Diseases*, p. 637, quote Lunacy Commission tables showing that of 136,478 admissions to asylums in England and Wales, heredity influence ascertained in only 20.5 per cent of admissions.

[2] Rosanoff, A. J. and Orr, Florence I., "A Study of Heredity in Insanity in the Light of the Mendelian Theory." *Bulletin No. 5*, Eugenics Record Office, Cold Spring Harbor, N. Y.

[3] Gowers, Wm. R., "Heredity and Disease," *Royal Society of Medicine*, 1909, vol. ii, p. 15.

[4] Lugaro, Ernesto, *Modern Problems in Psychiatry*, 1909 (trans. by D. Orr and R. G. Rows) emphasizes the fact that it is not a rare occurrence to see robust individuals spring from a marriage of weak individuals when the conditions of life are favorable. p. 212.

[5] Bateson, W., *Mendel's Principles of Heredity*, 1909, pp. 303-305.

[6] Davenport, Charles B., *Heredity in Relation to Eugenics*, 1911, points out in preface to book (p. 111) that a large amount of investigation will be required before it will be possible to take a definite stand, and that the advance thus far made is chiefly in getting a better method of study.

still too much speculation in the field of psychiatry as to the origin and course of certain psychoses to make it advisable to accept as final any of a number of theories that have been formulated to date. There is even the feeling among psychiatrists and students of heredity that the psychoses may represent disease processes rather than true heredity,[1] or that they represent abnormal variations unfitted for survival in the world as it is at present organized. Thomson, in his well-known volume on "Heredity," states

> It should be recognized that man has created around himself a social heritage which often evolves quickly, hurrying and pressing its creator, who cannot always keep pace with it. This is the frequent condition of mental disorder. The attempt to keep pace with the changes in environment—physical, biological, psychical and social, causes a strain that provokes disease.[2]

What is needed in order to determine tne actual bearing of heredity on insanity is the establishment of an organized research which would especially make a study of the descendents, normal and otherwise, of the insane confined in hospitals. From the studies already made we know that insane patients have had a poor heredity in a greater percentage of cases than has been the case among normal persons. The researches suggested must necessarily extend over a period of years and until they are inaugurated and completed, the more accurate knowledge of the relationship existing between heredity and insanity will remain at least partly unknown.[3]

[1] Myerson, Abraham, "Mental Disease in Families," *Mental Hygiene*, April, 1919, p. 239.

[2] Thomson, J. Arthur, *Heredity*, 1908, p. 253.

[3] During the year ending Sept. 30, 1910, in the New York State Hospitals, in the cases where positive information could be elicited, there was a reported history of insanity in 27 per cent of the male, and 32 per cent of the female patients. (White and Jeliffe, *Modern Treatment of Mental Disorders*, vol. i, p. 812.)

(b) *Alcohol.* Another essential cause of insanity is the excessive indulgence in alcohol, which produces the familiar picture of drunkenness, and such excesses if frequently repeated, are apt sooner or later to produce one or another of the alcoholic psychoses.[1] Chronic alcoholic addicts are often of a psychopathic constitution, congenital or acquired,[2] and are characterized by a gradually progressive dementia, with diminished capacity for work, faulty judgment, defective memory, moral deterioration, occasional delusions, and various nervous symptoms.[3]

In a study relating to the use and effect of alcohol in relation to the alcoholic psychoses, it was found that, (1) the drink habit leading to alcoholic insanity is usually formed in early life, males acquiring the habit earlier than females; (2) the average duration of the alcoholic habit prior to admission to the hospital for the insane is approximately 22 years among the males and 16 years among the females; (3) the liquors causing alcoholic insanity in New York State are principally whiskey and beer, the former appearing to be the principal factor in the majority of cases; (4) either regular or periodic drinking may lead to alcoholic insanity, more than three-fourths of the patients observed (464) having been regular drinkers prior to admission; (5) a fixed habit of excessive drinking with frequent intoxica-

[1] Kraepelin pointed out that 10 per cent of the patients in the asylums for the insane in the German Empire were committed on account of mental diseases due to alcohol. In some institutions the number was as high as 30 per cent, and even then these figures did not include numerous cases where alcohol was the exciting cause of the trouble, as in cases of mania, epilepsy and paresis. (Kraepelin, "Duty of the State in the Care of the Insane," trans. by Stewart Paton, *Amer. Jo. of Ins.*, 1900, p. 236.)

[2] Jacoby, Geo. W., *Unsound Mind*, 1918, p. 288.

[3] Diefendorf, A. Ross, *Clinical Psychiatry*, 1907, p. 288.

tion precedes the mental breakdown in a great majority of the cases.[1]

The spread of the prohibition movement throughout the country during the past decade has resulted, to some extent at least, in the decrease in the number of cases of alcoholic insanity admitted to the New York State Hospitals. The following figures indicate the gradual decrease in the percentage of cases of alcoholic insanity annually admitted from 1909 to 1916,[2] and now that the prohibition amendment to the Constitution has become law, a more substantial decrease may naturally be expected to follow. From October 1, 1908 to June 30, 1916, 58,011 patients were admitted to New York State hospitals.

TABLE 2. NUMBER OF CASES OF ALCOHOLIC INSANITY

Year.	All Admissions. Number.		Per cent of Total Admissions.	
	Male.	Female.	Male.	Female.
1909	526	145	15.2	4.6
1910	546	148	14.7	4.4
1911	530	173	14.1	5.0
1912	529	153	14.0	4.4
1913	535	155	13.5	4.2
1914	418	137	10.1	3.6
1915	321	111	7.8	2.9
1916 (9 months)	255	98	8.0	3.2

In the year 1917 there was an increase in the number of first admissions in alcoholic insanity, a total of 549, 437 males and 157 females, or 8.6 per cent of the total first ad-

[1] Pollock, Horatio M., *State Hospitals Bulletin*, Aug., 1915.

[2] Pollock, Horatio M., "Decline of Alcohol as a Cause of Insanity," *Psychiatric Bulletin*, vol. xi, Apr., 1917, no. 2, pp. 103-104.

missions being classified in this group. The reasons for the marked change in this particular year are not known.[1] For the year ending June 30, 1918, the percentage of alcoholic cases admitted was 7.3 per cent males, and 3.0 per cent females, the lowest rate since 1909.[2] A more marked decrease is expected to follow within the next few years.

(c) *Syphilis.* Syphilis appears as the essential cause of all cases of general paralysis and of cerebral syphilis, as well as of a large proportion of the cases of cerebral arteriosclerosis.[3] General paralysis hardly ever develops before from ten to twenty years after the primary syphilitic infection.[4] Not counting cases of arteriosclerosis, which are not always of syphilic origin, 19.4 per cent of all male first admissions and 7.0 per cent of all female first admissions to the New York State hospitals during a given year, occurred on the basis of syphilis as an essential cause.[5] For the year ending June 30. 1918, the cases of general paralysis which have been gradually increasing in recent years, showed a percentage of 13.4 of all first admissions.[6] It is now a recognized fact that without a previous syphilis there can be no paresis.[7] Syphilis is not a sole factor, however. Only a very small proportion of the persons who are syphilitic develop general paralysis, and in many, if not almost all cases of general paralysis it has been found that the patient has recently passed through a

[1] S. H. C., 29th A. R., 1916-1917, p. 407.

[2] S. H. C., 30th A. R., p. 285.

[3] De Fursac and Rosanoff, *op. cit.*, pp. 9-10.

[4] Kraepelin, *Clinical Psychiatry* (trans. by Thomas Johnstone), 1917, p. 41.

[5] S. H. C., 25th A. R., p. 312.

[6] S. H. C., 30th A. R., p. 284.

[7] Dercum, *Clinical Manual*, p. 256.

period of mental or other stress, which has seemed to determine the onset of the disease.[1]

(d) *Injuries and Other Causes.* Head injuries are responsible for but a small percentage of the cases admitted to the state hospitals. In 1918 there were only 15 cases thus admitted, 13 being men and 2 women. In 1917 there were but 18 cases.[2] These cases are far more often brought to general hospitals than to hospitals for the insane for reasons that are sufficiently obvious.

(e) *Contributing Causes.* As mentioned above there are a number of contributing causes of insanity which in themselves are not responsible for any large percentage of cases of insanity, but which have, however, become recognized as important contributing factors in the causation of insanity. A number of these factors have already been mentioned, and to them may be added bodily diseases;[3] overwork, rarely a cause in healthy persons;[4] and the group of physiological factors including puberty, the puerperal state,[5] the climacteric and senility, all of which are indirect strains to which the organism is subject, by reason of the more or less profound physiological commotions they arouse in the nervous system.[6]

VI. CLASSIFICATION OF MENTAL DISEASES

(a) *Introduction.* There has been much difficulty experienced in constructing a final standard classification of mental diseases, due largely to the question as to whether

[1] Mercier, *Textbook of Insanity*, p. 244.

[2] S. H. C., 30th A. R., p. 284.

[3] Mercier, *Textbook of Insanity*, pp. 21-22.

[4] Craig, Maurice, *Psychological Medicine*, p. 29.

[5] See Lugaro, *Modern Problems in Psychiatry*, pp. 275-276; also Mercier, *Crime and Criminals*, 1918, p. 195 for a discussion of the puerperal state and insanity.

[6] Church and Peterson, *Nervous and Mental Diseases*, p. 668.

such classification should be established on an etiological basis, on symptomatology, or from the point of view of pathological anatomy.[1] Various classifications have been proposed,[2] but the one followed in this work is the classification used in the New York State Hospitals and gradually being extended to all the hospitals for the insane in the United States.[3]

Table 3 follows the classification above alluded to and sets forth the psychoses, neuroses, and other ailments of Jewish admissions to the psychopathic wards of Bellevue Hospital for a period of a year. In order that this study may be intelligible to the layman as well as to the social worker, a brief discussion of the nature, prognosis and treatment of the various psychoses will accompany the consideration of the statistics presented. In accounting for the large number of males (673) admitted in comparison to the number of females (454) it should be noted that there are relatively more males in the foreign-born white population of the country than in the native-born white population; a ratio of 129.9 males to 100 females for the former compared with 102.7 to 100 for the latter.[4]

(b) *Senile Psychosis.* The senile psychoses, of which there were 16 male and 25 female admissions, are characterized by a gradually progressive mental deterioration accom-

[1] Diefendorf, A. Ross, *Clinical Psychiatry*, pp. 116-117.

[2] White, *Outlines of Psychiatry*, 1918, p. 19, suggests that the following be used: paranoia and paranoia states; manic-depressive psychoses; paresis, dementia praecox, senile and arteriosclerotic psychoses, infection exhaustion psychoses, toxic psychoses, those associated with organic diseases and injury of the brain, symptomatic psychoses, borderline states, and idocy and imbecility.

[3] *Vide Statistical Manual for the Use of Institutions for the Insane*, prepared by the American Medico-Psychological Association and the National Committee for Mental Hygiene (pamp. 40 pp.) 1918.

[4] *Insane and Feebleminded in Institutions*, Bureau of Census, 1914, p. 27.

TABLE 3. PSYCHOSES OF ADMISSIONS

Diagnosis.	Male.	Female.	Total.
Senile Psychosis	16	25	41
Arteriosclerosis	17	2	19
Organic Nervous Dis.	12	6	18
General Paralysis	88	11	99
General Paralysis, Juv.	1	..	1
Lues	1	..	1
Cerebral Syphilis	3	2	5
Chorea	1	1	2
Brain Tumor	4	..	4
Cerebral Hemorrhage	1	..	1
Chronic Alcoholism	17	2	19
Intoxication Psychoses	3	..	3
Toxic Delirium	1	..	1
Heroin Poisoning	2	6	8
Infection Exhaustion	4	13	17
Manic Depressive	102	103	205
Manic Depressive Mixed	35	54	89
Allied to Man. Dep.	30	32	62
Involution Melancholia	1	5	6
Dementia Praecox, Para.	44	34	78
Dementia Praecox, Kata.	5	1	6
Dementia Praecox, Hebe.	118	34	152
Dementia Praecox, Simple.	21	18	39
Dementia Praecox, Allied	19	24	43
Paranoid Conditions	8	2	10
Epilepsy	32	14	46
Psychoneurotic	4	..	4
Hysteria	1	9	10
Hysterical Episode	1	1	2
Constitutional Infer.	21	9	30
Mental Defective	26	15	41
Imbecility	7	1	8
Depression Undiff.	1	17	18
Transitory Confusion	3	2	5
Hypomanic	..	1	1
Unclassified	7	1	8
Not Insane	16	9	25
Totals	673	454	1,127

panied by a series of lesions in the central nervous system.[1] The most conspicuous feature of these cases is a defect of memory, especially for more recent events,[2] and often an

[1] Diefendorf, p. 369.

[2] Mercier, *Textbook of Insanity*, p. 309.

outbreak of ill-temper. The course of the affection is progressive until death. The patients finally become completely demented so that they are wholly disorientated, confused, know no one around them; in fact may not even know their own names.[1] The disease is encountered most frequently between sixty and seventy-five years of age; individuals with a faulty constitutional endowment, worn with hardships, and especially those addicted to excesses, may succumb before sixty.

(c) *Arteriosclerosis.* Arteriosclerosis was the diagnosis in the cases of 17 males and 2 females. This disease is not, as some have thought, always of syphilitic origin or affection,[2] but may also be brought on by gout, lead poisoning, alcoholism, pulmonary and cardiac conditions.[3] Among the physical symptoms are headaches, insomnia, muscular weakness, attacks of faintness or dizziness, epileptiform or apoplectiform seizures. The mental symptoms indicate diminished capacity for work, undue fatigability, emotional instability and depression; later, forgetfulness and general mental deterioration. The course of the disease in most cases extends over a number of years, even ten or twenty years. The prognosis is unfavorable for recovery, though under favorable conditions, such as rest, freedom from worry or excitement, moderation in eating and drinking, the condition may remain approximately stationary for months or even years.[4] A study of the New York State Hospital statistics has shown that the senile and arteriosclerotic, as well as the paretic groups, have high rates of first admis-

[1] White, *Outlines of Psychiatry*, p. 183.

[2] De Fursac and Rosanoff, p. 444.

[3] Church and Peterson, p. 195.

[4] De Fursac and Rosanoff, pp. 448, 452.

sions and deaths, with low rates of readmissions and discharges.[1]

(d) *Organic Nervous Diseases.* Psychic disorders induced by pathologic processes in the brain, such as meningitis, tumor, softening, and hemorrhage, are included under the category of organic nervous diseases. Emotional irritability, hallucinations of the various senses, defects of intelligence, and stuporous conditions are common mental manifestations of these processes. Eighteen such cases were admitted, 12 males and 6 females.

(e) *General Paralysis.* Some consideration has already been given to syphilis as a cause of mental disease, and from the figures in Table 3, it is seen that there were 99 cases of general paralysis, 88 males, 11 females and one case of juvenile general paralysis, all of which were a result of syphilis.[2] About 9 per cent of Jewish admissions were directly traceable to syphilis as the cause of the mental disease;[3] this includes the juvenile case, which developed years after the primary infection.[4] Studies of recent immigration, that is, prior to 1914, indicate that three-fourths of

[1] *Psychiatric Bulletin*, vol. ii, no. iv, Oct., 1917, New York State Hospital Statistics. Death rate per 1,000 patients under treatment in principal groups of psychoses in civil state hospitals for 1918 was as follows: general paralysis 352.8, cerebral arteriosclerosis 340.2, senile 297.2, these being three highest figures. (S. H. C., 30th A. R., p. 312.)

[2] For a comprehensive and thorough study of general paralysis, *vide* Kraepelin, "General Paresis," *Nervous and Mental Disease Mongographs*, series no. 14.

[3] General paralysis constituted 13.4 per cent of all first admissions to the New York State Hospitals for the year ending June 30, 1918. (S. H. C., 30th A. R., p. 284.)

[4] Stokes, John H., *The Third Great Plague*, 1917, presents a satisfactory discussion of the whole question of syphilis and its effects upon society. See also Vedder, Edward B., *Syphilis and Public Health*, 1918, Salmon, Thomas W., "General Paralysis as a Public Health Problem," *Amer. Jo. of Ins.*, 1914-1915, pp. 45-50.

the married men, excepting Jews, among the immigrants left their wives in Europe, and that nearly 85 per cent of all the males of the Slavic and Italian races living in the United States are single or are married men living here apart from their wives.[1] This has resulted in conditions which have a very definite bearing upon the prevalence of venereal diseases.[2] Paresis is relatively more common in cities than in rural districts,[3] and yet among Jewish immigrants who bring their wives with them intending to remain, but who also congregate in the cities, general paralysis is less prevalent than among the native population.[4]

Paretics are thus diagnosed because they become absent-minded, do not grasp events transpiring about them, mistake persons and objects, and lose themselves among familiar surroundings.[5] An increased tendency to fatigue is frequently among the first symptoms of the disease, the patient finding his ordinary labor very difficult. Paretics seldom have a true realization of their condition. On the contrary, the patients frequently feel healthier than previously, or, at least, they do not appreciate that they have lost all their mental powers. In the patient's behavior there is a noticeable bluntness to the demands of propriety and custom which leads him to exhibitions of tactlessness, lack of restraint and even gross offenses, without his having the least realization thereof. They are careless of appearance,

[1] White and Jelliffe, *Modern Treatment of Mental and Nervous Disorders*, vol. i, p. 255.

[2] Kraepelin and other authorities have pointed out that unmarried persons seem to be more prone to paresis than the married. (See Kraepelin, "General Paresis," p. 149.)

[3] Dercum, *Clinical Manual*, p. 258.

[4] White and Jelliffe, vol. i, p. 255.

[5] Kraepelin, "General Paresis," p. 1.

have no sense of order or cleanliness, boast obtrusively, and disclose their most intimate affairs.[1]

The disease may be said to be absolutely fatal, and occasional alleged cures should be regarded with the greatest skepticism.[2] The acute forms of the disease are rapidly fatal, the majority die in from eighteen months to three years, while in a certain few cases the disease process is very slow and may occupy many years.[3] Of the 99 cases admitted, 73 males and 11 females were committed to state hospitals; of the remaining male patients 12 were taken home by relatives, one, a well-known actor, was sent to a private sanatorium, where he died within a few days, and two died in the psychopathic ward.

Table 4 indicates the years during which general paralysis usually appears, and brings out the fact that about 66 per cent of the cases occur between the ages of 35 and 50 years, the busiest and undoubtedly the most fruitful years of the lives of active men and women.

TABLE 4. AGE DISTRIBUTION: GENERAL PARALYSIS

Age.	Male.	Female.	Totals.
20–24	2	1	3
25–29	4	2	6
30–34	7	4	11
35–39	17	..	17
40–44	29	2	31
45–49	16	1	17
50–54	7	1	8
55–59	3	..	3
60 and over	3	..	3
Totals	88	11	99

1 Kraepelin, "General Paresis," pp. 3, 12, 15.

2 *Ibid.*, p. 96.

3 Dercum, *Clinical Manual*, p. 258.

In the treatment of general paralysis, institutional care from the first seems to be pre-eminently essential. The patient is absolutely unable to care for himself and in a great majority of instances the friends are equally unable to care for him. As soon as the diagnosis is made steps should be taken looking towards the appointment of a committee of his person and property or otherwise guarding his business interests, if any; upon investigation such interests show, almost without fail, evidences of poor management, the result of early manifestations of the dementia.[1]

The economic loss to the State of New York on account of syphilitic mental disease for one year is sufficiently large to compel attention, especially since it is recognized that prompt treatment during the first stages of syphilitic infection would remove the danger of the involvement of the nervous system. Dr. Horatio M. Pollock, statistician of the New York State Hospital Commission, and a very careful and competent student of the subject, has made the following computations:

Cost of maintenance of patients in institutions	$471,918.72
Loss of earnings of males	4,652,942.35
Loss of earnings of females	273,783.92
Total loss	$5,398,644.99

When it is remembered that patients with syphilitic mental diseases rarely, if ever, recover and that death occurs on the average within two years of the time of entrance in the hospitals, it would seem that humanitarian considerations alone would impel city and state authorities to do everything within their power to check the ravages of syphilis. Moreover, the enormous economic loss due to syphilitic mental diseases furnishes a financial argument that can not well be ignored.[2]

[1] White, *Outlines of Psychiatry*, pp. 138-139.

[2] Pollock, "Economic Loss on Account of Syphilitic Mental Diseases," *Mental Hygiene*, Apr., 1918, pp. 277-282.

(f) *Juvenile General Paralysis.* Juvenile general paralysis is usually due to inherited syphilis, though it may have its origin in syphilis acquired in infancy; compared with the adult form it is of course, rare.[1] Although but comparatively few cases of general paralysis in children have been reported, it undoubtedly occurs quite frequently but is usually unrecognized. The possibility of general paralysis should be thought of in all cases of progressive mental impairment in children.[2] The single case referred to in Table 3 was that of an eight year old boy whose mother, still living, had contracted syphilis from the child's father sixteen years prior to admission of the youngster to the hospital; the mother was treated with mercury for six years and pronounced cured; she gave birth to no other children, though she had several miscarriages and re-married on the death of the child's father. The patient was treated with salvarsan for two years, as well as with mercury for many months; despite the vigorous course of treatment the Wasserman tests continued to indicate four plus. At the state hospital staff meeting when this case came up for diagnosis and discussion the question as to whether or not the patient belonged in a state hospital for the insane was considered, but due to the fact that no other institution would receive him, he still remains in the state hospital among adults.[3] Kraepelin has pointed out that among the cases of juvenile general paralysis of the female sex coming to his attention, the patients are strikingly often prostitutes.[4]

[1] Dercum, *Clinical Manual,* p. 259.

[2] White, *Outlines of Psychiatry,* p. 132.

[3] Miller, Henry W. and Achucarro, N., reported a somewhat similar case—that of a boy 12 years of age, illegitimate, mother had syphilis before birth of child but refused to undergo treatment; also had several miscarriages. (*Amer. Jo. of Ins.,* Jan., 1911, pp. 559-570.)

[4] Kraepelin, "General Paresis," p. 153.

(g) *Lues and Cerebral Syphilis.* Lues, another name for syphilis, presented only one case that found its way to the psychopathic ward. There were five cases of cerebral syphilis, 3 males and 2 females. Of the males, one was a married man of 34, who had been treated in several hospitals, and whom it became necessary to send to the City Hospital, his mental condition being sufficiently intact to render him a non-committable case.[1] The other patient was also a married man, aged 32, who was being kept at home while receiving the salvarsan treatment at one of the semi-private hospitals.[2] One of the women, aged 31, single, came from Randall's Island and died in the ward within ten days after admission. The other, a married woman of 46, was taken home by her husband after her mental condition had somewhat cleared up. Cerebral syphilis is not so often met with as general paralysis, at least in psychopathic wards or hospitals for the insane. For the year ending June 30, 1918, there were 913 cases of general paralysis admitted to the New York State Hospitals, and only 49 cases of cerebral syphilis thus admitted.[3] This is a grave affection; untreated cases progress more or less rapidly with tissue destruction and often a fatal termination. Treatment, however, if instituted early, may result in a quick and apparently perfect cure, the treatment being that of syphilis in general.[4]

(h) *Chorea.* Two cases of chorea were admitted, one

[1] The City Hospital of the Department of Public Charities of the City of New York receives patients suffering from syphilis in its various forms, and for whom no other provision can be made.

[2] In this study when a patient is readmitted during the year to the psychopathic ward, each admission is considered as though it were a separate admission.

[3] S. H. C., 30th A. R., p. 410.

[4] De Fursac and Rosanoff, pp. 442-443.

male and one female; the former, a youth of 19 years, arrested, charged with a felony, and sent to the hospital for observation, thereafter being returned to the city prison. The second case was that of a married woman 33 years of age, whom it was necessary to commit to a state hospital. The abnormal mental conditions occurring as a part of chorea have been found to be an immediate cause of delinquency,[1] the coincidence in this single case being instructive. Huntington's chorea, the diagnosis in the second case, usually sets in between the ages of 35 and 50 years.[2] It is a chronic, slowly progressive, incurable affection, mental symptoms appearing in almost every case sooner or later, with a weakness of judgment, general dissatisfaction with surroundings, a growing selfishness and irritability being among the earliest symptoms observed.[3] Studies of family histories have indicated that every sufferer from this form of chorea had at least one affected parent, the obvious way in which this disease can be eliminated being for those who suffer from it not to have children.[4]

(i) *Brain Tumor.* In many cases of brain tumor the symptoms are not of a sufficiently pronounced character to render their recognition easy,[5] though they are often limited to headache, vomiting, vertigo, optic neuritis, together with certain neurological conditions depending upon which portion of the brain is affected. In about two-thirds of all cases mental phenomena are added.[6] Of the four men ad-

[1] White and Jelliffe, vol. i, pp. 221-222.

[2] De Fursac and Rosanoff, pp. 360-361.

[3] Hamilton, A. S., "A Report of Twenty-seven Cases of Chronic Progressive Chorea," *Amer. Jo. of Ins.*, Jan., 1908, pp. 403-474.

[4] White and Jelliffe, vol. i, pp. 33-34.

[5] Paton, Stewart, *Psychiatry*, p. 458.

[6] Dercum, *Clinical Manual*, p. 291.

mitted, all were between 35 and 40 years of age; two were discharged to the custody of relatives, one was committed to a state hospital, and the fourth died on the ward within three days after admission, having been brought to the hospital in a moribund condition.

(j) *Cerebral Hemorrhage.* The single case of cerebral hemorrhage was that of a man 43 years of age, who had been struck on the head by a bar of iron while at his work. He left the hospital within a day after admission, and his condition had not fully cleared up months later, especially as it was aggravated by heavy drinking of alcoholic liquors. He was not considered a proper case for commitment.

(k) *Alcoholism.* The question of alcoholism and the problems it creates has been discussed in preceding pages. Many writers have pointed out that Jews contribute but a small percentage of alcoholic psychoses to the total admissions to state hospitals.[1] Of the 22 admissions for which alcohol was the essential cause, but 3 cases presented an acute alcoholic psychosis, these being the only alcoholics to be subsequently committed to a hospital, one to a private sanatorium, 2 to a state hospital, out of a total of 828 commitments,[2] while 5.2 per cent of first admissions for the state as a whole presented alcoholic psychoses.[3]

(l) *Narcotic Drug Poisoning.* During the past few years the number of cases of narcotic drug poisoning has increased very perceptibly and the nine cases of drug poisoning including one of toxic delirium, represent only those whom it was found advisable temporarily to detain in the

[1] Fishberg, Maurice, *The Jews*, pp. 273-274, 342-43; Kirby, George H., "Race and Alcoholic Insanity," *Jo. Amer. Med. Assn.*, July 1, 1911, pp. 9-11; Swift, H. M., "Insanity and Race," *Amer. Jo. of Ins.*, July, 1913, p. 152.

[2] See table 14, "Disposition of Patients."

[3] S. H. C., 30th A. R., p. 285.

psychopathic wards.[1] None of these cases required commitment to a state hospital though the existence of proper and adequate facilities would have helped materially in the treatment of these and many other patients suffering similarly.

(m) *Infection Exhaustion Psychosis.* All factors capable of bringing about rapid and profound exhaustion of the organism occur in the etiology of primary mental confusion; physical and mental stress, painful and prolonged emotions, but especially grave somatic affections. The puerperal state, through the exhaustion which it entails as well as through the nutritive disorders and infections by which it is sometimes complicated; infectious diseases (typhoid, influenza, cholera); profuse hemorrhages, *etc.* are among the causes frequently found in the history of the disease. Out of a total of 13 female cases of infection exhaustion psychosis, 6 resulted from the puerperal state, 5 from pneumonia, 1 from chronic cardiac disease, 1 from blood poisoning. Four male cases were recorded, 1 resulting from pulmonary tuberculosis, 2 from pneumonia, and 1 from empyema.

(n) *Manic Depressive Insanity.* The largest single group of cases to be admitted was the manic depressive which totaled 356 patients, or about 31 per cent of the total admissions. The term "manic depressive insanity" was introduced by Kraepelin[2] and is in general use at present to signify cases in which the attacks present a double characteristic: a tendency towards recovery without in-

[1] For a discussion of the problem of drug addiction in New York, with special reference to Jewish drug addicts, see Goldberg, Jacob A., *The Drug Habit as a Social and Legislative Problem* (M. A. thesis, Columbia Univ., 1916).

[2] Dercum, *Clinical Manual*, p. 64; also, Kraepelin, *Lehrbuch der Psychiatrie*, band ii.

tellectual enfeeblement and a tendency toward recurrency.[1] The principal cause is hereditary taint, and it is noteworthy that this disease is often found in families, the constitutional condition as the basis on which it develops appearing to be directly transmitted.[2] From a symptomatic standpoint the attacks are of three types: manic, presenting a flight of ideas, irritability, and motor excitement; depressed, with psychic inhibition, and a painful emotional state associated with indifference; mixed, in which a period of depression and period of excitement alternate, the transition being either sudden or gradual.[3] It has been found that this psychosis occurs more frequently in females than in males, about in proportion of 2 to 1.[4] Of the cases under consideration, the males in this group accounted for 24.8 per cent of the total male admissions, whereas for the females, 41.6 per cent of the admissions were classified as manic depressive insanity. The individual attacks vary in duration from a few days to several months, some attacks, however, being greatly prolonged.[5] Recovery from the single attack is the rule, while the likelihood of subsequent attacks is usually presumed to be quite certain. The prognosis of the disease is bad as to ultimate recovery though good for the separate attacks.[6]

[1] De Fursac and Rosanoff, p. 293; also White and Jelliffe, vol. i, p. 535.

[2] White, Wm. A., *Outlines of Psychiatry*, p. 99; Peterson, Frederick, *Mental Diseases*, 1899, p. 694, holds that hereditary taint is found in 75 per cent and degenerative stigmata in 20 per cent of cases.

[3] White and Jelliffe, vol. i, pp. 529-589 present a thorough discussion of this psychosis.

[4] Dercum, p. 63.

[5] A most interesting study of a case of manic depressive insanity lasting for many months is described by Clifford W. Beers in "A Mind that Found Itself," being a detailed story of the attack suffered by Mr. Beers.

[6] Readmissions to the state hospitals are indicated in table 22.

In the accompanying table, the manic and depressed cases are not separated, the total admissions having been 102 males, 103 females; of mixed psychoses 35 were males and 54 females. It is often difficult to draw a sharp line between borderline cases, and these have been entered as allied to manic depressive insanity, 30 males and 32 females.[1] The following table points out the final disposition of the cases in this group.

TABLE 5. DISPOSITION OF M. D. I. PATIENTS

Disposition.	Male.	Female.	Totals.
State Hospitals	135	159	294
Private Sanatoria	11	15	26
Returned to City Prison	2	..	2
Discharged	19	15	34
Totals	167	189	356

These figures, indicating a large number of commitments and but a few discharges, usually of borderline cases or those whom relatives insisted on taking home, help bring to the fore a marked weakness in the system of care and treatment of the insane. Many, if not a majority of these patients would have recovered from the attack if cared for in a psychopathic hospital for a period of a few weeks. Instead, they were sent to an overcrowded and undermanned state hospital in which facilities for the treatment of these so-called acute cases are below the necessary minimum. It is because of the lack of an essential link (psychopathic hospital) in the state hospital system that much of the

[1] On the early differential diagnosis between dementia praecox and manic depressive insanity, *vide* Dercum, *Penn. Med. Jo.*, Aug., 1917, p. 765.

overcrowding is due. Given such hospitals in different parts of the state, a marked percentage of the present overcrowded conditions would be eliminated within a short space of time.

The distribution of cases of manic depressive insanity according to age was as follows:

Table 6. Age Distribution of M. D. I. Patients

Age.	Male.	Female.	Totals.
Under 15	3	4	7
15–19	15	32	47
20–24	39	45	84
25–29	32	32	64
30–34	20	29	49
35–39	23	21	44
40 and over	35	26	61
Totals	167	189	356

As in the cases of dementia praecox (Table 8), the outstanding feature of the above figures is the comparative youthfulness of the majority of cases. In this group there is a larger proportion of those over 30 years of age, due to a number of causes, among those being the fact that dementia praecox psychoses develop earlier than manic depressive attacks, and also to the fact that many of the more serious stresses in life do not come till after the thirtieth year, heredity and stress being, as aforementioned, the most important causes of manic depressive psychoses. Over 82 per cent of the above cases were under 40 years of age, in the very prime of life, and irrespective of the sadness and misery resulting, the economic loss to society as a result of this must in any event be very large.

(o) *Involutional Melancholia.* Involutional melancholia, the diagnosis in 1 male and 5 female cases, occurs chiefly after forty-five years of age. The ages of the six patients were 42, 45, 53, 54, 56 and 60 years. The causes of this disease are not well known, though a neuropathic heredity has been found in about 60 per cent of the cases.[1] Among the symptoms are anorexia, insomnia, irritability, unwarranted pessimism, a tendency to rapid fatigue, with often a marked depression, leading in a number of cases to suicide, unless closely guarded. It was found necessary to commit each of the six patients to a state hospital.

(p) *Dementia Praecox.* Dementiá praecox, one of the commonest forms of mental disease, is a psychosis essentially of the period of puberty and adolescence, characterized by mental deterioriation tending to progress, though frequently interrupted by remissions. According to Kraepelin sixty per cent of all cases of dementia praecox begin before the twenty-fifth year, the simple form usually starting between the fifteenth and twenty-fifth year, the paranoid form beginning around the end of the second decade, and one-half of the katatonic cases setting in around the twenty-fifth year.[2] It is to Kraepelin that much credit belongs for the great interest taken in the subject of dementia praecox in recent years, due to the serious effort on his part to clear up the early confusion.[3] There were 212 males and 117 females admitted to the psychopathic wards in one year, the largest number being among the hebephrenic form, of whom 118 males and 34 females came to the hospital. The real significance and importance of the cases of dementia praecox from the point of view of hospital expenditures and management especially, may be gathered from the fact that on July 1, 1916, 53.81 per cent of the patients in all the

[1] De Fursac and Rosanoff, p. 324.

[2] Jacoby, *Unsound Mind*, p. 197.

[3] Hall, G. Stanley, *Adolescence*, 1908, vol. i, p. 301.

state hospitals for the insane in New York were diagnosed as dementia praecox, whereas the psychosis that stood next highest was the manic depressive group and the allied forms thereof, of which there were less than 10 per cent.[1] In 1917 the proportion of dementia praecox cases was 53.8 per cent,[2] and in 1918 it rose to 58.7 per cent.[3] The financial burden which the state must carry in caring for these patients is increasing from year to year, and the need to find a way out is very urgent, since with better care, improved diet and housing conditions, the length of life of these patients in the institutions tends to increase, and thus the percentage of such patients will naturally increase as time goes on.

There are many difficulties however, in discovering ways and means of curing or so improving the mental condition of dementia praecox patients that they may safely be discharged from custody. To begin with, only the outward manifestations of the disease are known with any degree of accuracy, whereas the causes are almost completely unknown.[4] It is generally agreed that probably the most important question in contemporary psychiatry is the nature of dementia praecox, that is, the genesis of the disease process.[5] There have been many theories advanced as to the cause and nature of the disease. Some have held that heredity is to be regarded as the essential cause of the disorder;[6] that heredity plays an uncertain role in its

[1] *Psychiatric Bulletin*, Oct., 1917, p. 456.

[2] S. H. C., 29th A. R., p. 440.

[3] S. H. C., 30th A. R., p. 292.

[4] Tanzi, Eugenio, *Textbook of Mental Diseases*, 1909, pp. 663-665.

[5] Coriat, Isidor H., "Psychopathology of Dementia Praecox," *Amer. Jo. of Ins.*, Jan., 1917, pp. 670-671; Southard, E. E., "A Study of Dementia Praecox," *Amer. Jo. of Ins.*, July, 1910, pp. 124-125.

[6] De Fursac and Rosanoff, p. 280.

etiology;[1] that abnormal functions of internal glands are responsible for the disorder;[2] that dementia praecox is dependent upon an auto-intoxication produced by poisons which are elaborated in the sexual organs and which are especially injurious to the brain;[3] that infectious diseases, especially influenza, may become the starting point of dementia praecox.[4] From the varied and conflicting views it is quite apparent that much still remains to be discovered regarding dementia praecox, though certain more or less definite facts concerning the various manifestations of the different forms of the disease have been determined.[5]

Parents and relatives of children who begin to show symptoms of dementia praecox rarely understand the reasons for the apparent laziness, their inability to apply themselves to their studies or work, the irritability and failure to join in the games and sports of their fellows.[6]

[1] White, *Outlines of Psychiatry*, p. 140.

[2] Hoch, August, "Precipitating Mental Causes in Dementia Praecox," *Amer. Jo. of Ins.*, Jan., 1914, p. 637; Auer, E. Murray, "Disease of the Glands of Internal Secretion," *Amer. Jo. of Ins.*, Oct., 1914, p. 498.

[3] Tanzi, *op. cit.*, pp. 663-665, quotes Kraepelin on this point; Tanzi disagrees with this theory.

[4] Paton, *Psychiatry*, p. 405.

[5] Abbott, E. S., "Meyer's Theory of the Psychogenic Origin of Dementia Praecox," *Amer. Jo. of Ins.*, July, 1911, pp. 15-22, makes the observation that causes are multiple, and so diligent search is necessary, not only along psychobiological lines, as advised by Meyer, but in others, including all possible organic changes as well. For a further discussion of Meyer's theory see *Psychological Clinic*, vol. ii, p. 92 *et seq.*; *Amer. Jo. of Psychology*, vol. xxi, p. 395 *et seq.*

[6] Flexner, Bernard and Baldwin, Roger N., *Juvenile Courts and Probation*, 1914, pp. 41-42, advise the establishment of psychopathic clinics attached to public schools in order to discover these cases at an early stage of their illness. MacCurdy, John T., "Psychiatric Clinics in the Schools," *Amer. Jo. of Public Health*, vol. vi, no. xii, pp. 1265-1270, points out why psychiatric clinics in the schools may offer reasonable hope of reducing insanity in the latter life of the pupils. *Vide* Healy, William, *The Individual Delinquent*, 1915, pp. 66-67.

The result is that these potential cases of dementia praecox are kept at home until the disease is fully developed and the patience of their relatives is exhausted, when they are brought to the psychopathic ward for commitment to a state hospital. The following figures show the large proportion of the cases that were committed:

TABLE 7. DISPOSITION OF CASES OF D. P.

Disposition.	Male.	Female.	Totals.
State Hospitals	174	105	279
Private Sanatoria	6	2	8
Children's Society	..	1	1
City Prison	4	..	4
Died on Ward	1	..	1
Discharged	27	9	36
Totals	212	117	329

It has been computed that dementia praecox involves annual direct and indirect losses to the State of New York of more than $10,000,000.[1] This is largely so because these cases remain in the state hospitals for an average of 16 years, most of them being of wage-earning age, as seen from the figures that follow:

TABLE 8. AGE DISTRIBUTION OF D. P. PATIENTS

Age.	Male.	Female.	Totals.
Under 15	2	2	4
15-19	40	15	55
20-24	61	17	78
25-29	55	31	86
30-34	27	20	47
35-39	15	13	28
40 and over	12	19	31
Totals	212	117	329

[1] Pollock, "Dementia Praecox as a Social Problem," *State Hospital Quarterly*, Aug., 1918.

The fact that the recovery rate of dementia praecox patients in state hospitals is very low,[1] is an additional contributing factor to the high percentage of such cases in institutions, outnumbering, as they do, all other patients put together. Merely to herd these cases in state hospitals is a hopeless task and further steps must be taken either by the state or by private agencies, or by both, to find ways and means of solving the problem of proper and advisable methods to be pursued in the study, care and treatment of this group of the state's charges.

(q) *Paranoid Conditions.* Paranoia is a chronic progressive psychosis occurring mostly in early adult life, between the ages of 25 and 40 years, characterized by the gradual development of a stable progressive system of delusions without marked mental deterioration, clouding of consciousness, or disorder of thought, will or conduct.[2] The disease is not common, and constitutes only a small percentage of the cases admitted to insane asylums.[3] Men are more often afflicted than women. It develops on a defective constitutional basis, either congenital or acquired, defective heredity existing in a very large percentage of the cases.[4] The development of the psychosis is often slow and gradual, though it may develop very rapidly, almost suddenly.[5] The patient will usually change in disposition,

[1] Pollock, "A Statistical View of Mental Disease in the New York State Hospitals" *Psychiatric Bulletin*, Oct., 1917.

[2] Diefendorf, *op. cit.*, p. 420.

[3] In 1918 only 4.4 per cent of the patients in the New York State Hospitals were suffering from paranoiac conditions. (S. H. C., 30th A. R., p. 292.)

[4] Dercum, *Clinical Manual*, maintains that heredity is responsible in 85 to 90 per cent of cases. (p. 134.)

[5] A difference of opinion exists as to the rapidity of onset. Thus De Fursac and Rosanoff (p. 287) maintain that the rapid development of the disease is more frequent, whereas Diefendorf (p. 424) holds that

become somewhat irritable, grumbling, very suspicious, and easily discontented. There were but 10 such cases admitted, 8 males and 2 females; 7 were taken home by relatives and 3 committed to state hospitals.[1] Practically all writers on the subject agree as to the chronicity and incurability of paranoia;[2] and though a few recoveries have been reported, a critical examination of these cases has resulted in a disagreement as to the diagnosis.[3]

(r) *Epilepsy and Mental Deficiency.* Among the remainder of the Jewish cases brought to the psychopathic ward, there were 32 male and 14 female epileptics, and 33 male and 16 female mental defectives of all kinds. Bad heredity is by far the most common and important cause of the above mental conditions, though parental alcoholism and parental syphilis are additional important factors.[4] Most of the patients of this group were brought to the

the onset is very gradual, extending sometimes over years. If the Freudian view is taken, namely, that paranoia is a defense psychosis determined by the nature of the painful reminiscences repressed, then the latter view must be accepted. *Vide* Freud, E., *Selected Papers on Hysteria and other Psychoneuroses*, 1909, pp. 165-174.

[1] Kirby, George H., "Dementia Praecox, Paraphrenia and Paranoia," *Amer. Jo. of Ins.*, vol. lxxi, p. 359, states that paranoia is the outgrowth of personal difficulties in the adaptation to the environment of abnormally constituted personalities, and that most of these cases are able to get along in society and their commitment is usually not necessary.

[2] Abbott, E. S., "What is Paranoia," *Amer. Jo. of Ins.*, vol. lxxi, p. 41.

[3] Bjerre, Paul, *History and Practice of Psychoanalysis* (pp. 205-246), presents the case of a paranoical system of persecution of ten years standing which he claims was entirely broken up and not a trace of recurrence appeared six years after conclusion of the treatment, which followed the psychoanalytic method and was extended over a long period of time. White, *Principles of Psychiatry*, p. 97, believes there are possibilities of accomplishing cures by attacking the problem therapeutically, probably along the lines followed by Bjerre.

[4] Tredgold, A. F., *Amentia*, offers a comprehensive study of this group of cases.

hospital either because they were sent by the courts for mental examination after arrest for some crime, or because relatives could no longer keep them at home. Only a few of these patients were committed to a state hospital, this step being taken only when they suffered from a psychosis in addition to the other condition. A majority of them should have been placed in institutions for the epileptic or feebleminded years prior to their arrest or hospital admission.[1] However, due to the failure of early diagnosis as well as to the overcrowded institutional conditions, these patients have been permitted to wander about the streets, fall into criminal ways, eventually to be sent to jails and prisons instead of to farm or industrial colonies in which they properly belong.[2] Until the state completes a comprehensive plan for the care of all such cases needing custodial or other similar care and treatment, no abatement of hospital and prison admissions of this group can properly be expected.

(s) *Psychoneuroses.* There were 4 cases of psychoneuroses, few of which find their way to the psychopathic wards and state hospitals, though neuroses constitute one of the most wide-spread forms of disease;[3] of hysteria 1 male and 9 female patients, and of hysterical episode 1 male and 1 female; of hypomanic 1 female; of various undifferen-

[1] Gesell, Arnold, "Mental Hygiene and the Public School," *Mental Hygiene*, Jan., 1919, pp. 4-10, suggests the means to be employed in public schools in order to pick out those children who are predisposed to mental or nervous conditions. Campbell, C. Macfie, "A City School District and Its Subnormal Children," *Mental Hygiene*, April, 1918, pp. 232-244, offers suggestions for constructive work with such children.

[2] Glueck, Bernard, "Types of Delinquent Careers," *Mental Hygiene*, April, 1917, pp. 171-195, shows how bad heredity and mental defectiveness may result in delinquent careers. *Vide* Glueck, "Concerning Prisoners," *Mental Hygiene*, April, 1918, pp. 177-218. Glueck, *Studies in Forensic Psychiatry*, 1916.

[3] White and Jelliffe, vol. i, p. 333.

tiated depressions, 1 male and 17 females; and of transitory confusion 3 males and 2 females. Eight cases, 7 males and 1 female were unclassified, due largely to the fact that they left the psychopathic ward in the custody of relatives before the examination could be made or completed.

(t) *Constitutional Inferiority.* Constitutional inferiority is a term applied to those who show a mildly dwarfed mental endowment with limited attainments and an inability to grapple with the problems of everyday life.[1] These cases are subject to episodes of excitement and depression, often developing paranoid states of a more or less transitory character. They frequently commit crimes and are essentially chronic in character, so far as duration is concerned. Many of them are never admitted to hospitals for the insane, but drift into prisons and reformatories, or other custodial institutions.[2] Their main difficulty seems to be in adjusting themselves to their environment but they cannot be regarded as mentally sick according to the definition of the code. It is for this reason that so many of them never reach a state hospital, and still in the various institutions to which they are sent they are unfortunately misunderstood and misjudged—the only solution of the difficulty seeming to be the creation of a special institution for those suffering from constitutional inferiority.[3]

Twenty-five cases admitted to the wards were found not to be insane and discharged to their own custody or turned over to police and court officials by whom they had been

[1] Karpas, Morris J., "Constitutional Inferiority," *Jo. Amer. Med. Assn.*, Dec. 16, 1916, p. 1831, presents an analysis of the concept of constitutional inferiority, especially regarding the method of diagnosis of such cases.

[2] White and Jelliffe, vol. i, pp. 846-847.

[3] Bellevue and Allied Hospitals, *Annual Report*, 1912, p. 64.

brought for mental examination upon order of a court. This completes the analysis from the point of view of diagnosis of the 1,127 Jewish cases admitted to Bellevue Hospital psychopathic wards. What follows immediately considers this group from different angles so that as complete a mental picture as possible may be obtained. In this way, it is hoped, the needs of the insane and the responsibility of the community towards them may be better understood and realized, and steps taken to alleviate and remedy conditions that should no longer be permitted to exist.

TABLE 9. NUMBER OF ADMISSIONS

	Male.	Female.	Total.
First Admissions	543	385	928
Readmissions	130	69	199
Totals	673	454	1,127

It is often difficult to ascertain whether or not certain patients admitted to the psychopathic wards are readmissions to these wards. The figures presented in Table 9, showing 17.6 per cent readmissions are undoubtedly low, especially in view of the much higher percentage of readmissions recorded in the state hospitals,[1] particularly as regards the Jewish patients under consideration. A number of these readmissions were parole cases from the state hospitals; others had been patients in state institutions whose parole period, formerly only six months but now, in some instances as long as one year, had expired, thus mak-

[1] S. H. C., 30th A. R., p. 278.

ing it necessary to have them recommitted. The question as to why so large a percentage of cases relapsed after discharge from the state hospitals will be considered in detail in another chapter.

VII. MARITAL CONDITION

In the following table (Table 10) the marital condition of the patients is presented. There were almost twice as many single as married males; whereas, of female patients, there were actually fewer single than married. The large percentage of single persons among the insane enumerated by the United States Census of 1910, showing 63.5 per cent male and 41.7 per cent female, compared to 60.3 per cent male and 44.5 per cent female in Table 10, should not be interpreted as indicating that the single are more liable to become insane than the married. It means rather, that the insane as compared with the normal are less likely to marry. That the percentage of single persons is smaller for females than for males, both among the insane and the general population, is due to the fact that women marry at a younger age than men. The psychoses which are largely responsible for the majority of cases of insanity do not as a rule develop until after the eighteenth year, except in the cases of dementia praecox, hebephrenic form. By this time in many cases, the females are married and for that reason psychoses were found to have developed in an unduly large number of young women whose marriage was a matter of but a short time. The added burdens of household care, of gestation, pregnancy, and lactation, have caused the onset of psychoses in persons as to whose good mental condition there was no question prior to marriage; at least the nearest relatives knew of no mental abnormality, indicated or latent.

The comparatively large number of married men and

women, many of them with dependent children, presents an important social problem. The majority of these patients were between the ages of 20 and 40 years, and the commitment of a father or mother to an institution for the insane left a family, in many cases, in straightened circumstances.

TABLE 10. MARITAL CONDITION

	Male.	Female.	Total.
Single	406	190	596
Married	234	201	435
Widowed	25	53	78
Divorced	8	10	18
Totals	673	454	1,127

With but very few exceptions, the social status of nearly all the patients was that of working people whose only source of income was what they themselves earned from week to week, or what relatives contributed out of meagre incomes. Under such conditions, the commitment of an unmarried young man or woman has in many cases meant a reduction in the family income, whereas in cases of married persons more serious adjustments have to be made, this often being possible only through the financial aid of a social or relief agency. The kind and amount of assistance to be rendered to such families depends on whether the father or the mother has been committed; the number and age of the children, if any; the financial resources of the family, and the assistance to be expected from relatives. Often the most important factor is the matter of the diagnosis of the patient; if a recovery may reasonably be expected within a few weeks or months, emergency assistance will usually be sufficient to keep the family together;

otherwise a more definite program of relief must be outlined and carried out.

VIII. NATIVITY

In the United States, and especially in New York State, the question of immigration in relation to insanity presents a problem of great magnitude. Of the total number of inmates of insane asylums on January 1, 1910, according to the enumeration of the Thirteenth Census, 28.8 per cent were whites of foreign birth, and of the persons admitted to such institutions during the year 1910, 25.5 per cent were of this class.[1] Of the total population of the United States in 1910 the foreign-born whites constituted 14.5 per cent.[2] The number of foreign born admitted to the New York State Hospitals for the year 1918 was 44.5 per cent of the total admissions; those of foreign parentage constituted 59.8 per cent and those of mixed parentage 11.0 per cent.[3] From this it seems that for the country as a whole and for New York State in particular the foreign born have an unduly large representation in insane asylums. However, it should be remembered that most cases of insanity occur after the eighteenth year, and that the difference in age distribution which exists between the native and foreign-born parts of the population accounts largely, but not wholly, for the difference in the proportion of insane hospital admissions.[4]

[1] *Insane and Feebleminded in Institutions*, U. S. Census, 1914, p. 48.

[2] *Ibid.*, p. 25.

[3] S. H. C., 30th A. R., p. 282.

[4] Rosanoff, A. J., "Some Neglected Phases of Immigration," *Amer. Jo. of Ins.*, July, 1915, p. 47; points out the apparent shortcomings in computing percentages without considering age distribution.

TABLE 11. NATIVITY

	Male.	Female.	Total.
Arabia	1	.	1
Austria-Hungary	127	115	242
Belgium	1	1	2
England	11	6	17
France	1	1	2
Germany	20	15	35
Greece	..	1	1
Palestine	1	..	1
Persia	..	1	1
Roumania	24	14	38
Russia	284	188	472
Spain	1	..	1
Switzerland	1	..	1
Turkey	4	2	6
Total	476	344	820
Native born	197	110	307
Totals	673	454	1,127

An unusually large number of the immigrants, especially the Jews, settle in the urban districts, more often in the larger cities. It is an established fact that an urban environment brings to the surface neuropathic tendencies of a community far more fully than a rural environment. Considering this factor together with the difference in age distribution, and making some allowance for the heavy stress entailed in the migration and in the subsequent process of adjustment to new conditions and more exacting standards of living, there is found to be but little difference, if any, between the native and foreign-born parts of the population in the incidence of certified insanity.[1]

Table 11 indicates that 820 or 72.7 per cent of the total

[1] De Fursac and Rosanoff, p. 19.

Jewish admissions under consideration were of foreign birth, and 307 or 27.3 per cent were native born. Russia contributed more than half of the foreign born, 284 males and 188 females, a total of 472; from Austria-Hungary came 127 males and 115 females, a total of 242; Roumania contributed a total of 38, Germany 35, England 17, Turkey 6, Belgium 2, France 2, and 1 each from Arabia, Greece, Palestine, Persia, Spain and Switzerland. The figures of admissions to the psychopathic wards indicate approximately the proportion of Jewish immigration from the various countries during recent years, especially the last 20 to 30 years prior to 1914. In view of what has been said on the matter of age distribution among immigrants and the fact that 72.7 per cent of admissions in one year were foreign-born, any seeming disproportion of insanity among Jews in the United States, particularly in New York, where most Jews live, must be discounted.[1] The further fact that nearly all Jewish immigrants settle in the cities, especially in the congested sections of the large seaboard communities, should render judgment still more cautious. From all available facts, the only conclusion that can be drawn indicates that there is no greater proneness toward mental disease in the foreign-born than in the native population and that the excessive proportion of hospital admissions furnished by the foreign-born is due to other causes.

IX. AGE DISTRIBUTION

Table 12 indicates the age distribution of the patients admitted. In interpreting the figures it should be remembered that the several clinical groups differ widely with respect to age distribution on admission. The senile and arterioscler-

[1] U. S. Census, *Population*, vol. i, p. 826, gives the foreign-born population in New York City in 1910 as 40.8 per cent of the total population; for the Borough of Manhattan, 47.9 per cent.

otic cases are found principally in the advanced age groups; the alcoholic, paretic and paranoiac cases occupy the middle-life groups; and the manic depressive (see Table 6) and dementia praecox (see Table 8) cases are most prominent in the age groups from 20 to 40 years.[1]

TABLE 12. AGE DISTRIBUTION

	Male.	Female.	Total,
Under 15 years	7	9	16
15–19	98	61	159
20–24	120	85	205
25–29	107	73	180
30–34	72	66	138
35–39	80	50	130
40–44	63	21	84
45–49	41	25	66
50–54	29	24	53
55–59	11	8	19
60–64	18	7	25
65 and over	27	25	52
Totals	673	454	1,127

For the country as a whole in the comparison of native and foreign born insane according to age distribution, the contrast is less striking in individual age groups than it is in the total population. For all ages combined the ratio is twice as large as it is for the native; but there is no such disproportion between the ratios in any one of the age groups.[2]

X. DEPORTATION OF IMMIGRANT INSANE

A circumstance which may have some influence upon the ratio of admissions to hospitals for the insane in the case

[1] The same distribution of clinical groups in the indicated age-groups is general for the entire state. (S. H. C., 30th A. R., p. 297.)

[2] *Insane and Feebleminded in Institutions*, U. S. Census, 1914, p. 26.

of the foreign born is the fact that under the present immigration laws the insane among immigrants are debarred from entering the United States, or if insanity develops within five years after entrance, are liable to be deported. Thus it might be said that as regards insanity, the foreign-born remaining in the United States are to a certain extent a selected class, and that so far as the influence of this one factor goes, there should be less insanity among them than among the native population. The Bureau of Deportation of the New York State Hospital Commission brought about the deportation of the following numbers of aliens: in 1914, 825; 1915, 490; 1916, 208; 1917, 52; and 1918, 53.[1] Had it not been for the commencement of hostilities in Europe and the consequent practical impossibility of carrying out deportation proceedings to any extent after July, 1914, the last year would probably have recorded about 900 deportations. Whether the larger number of these 900 aliens was insane or of neuropathic constitution, the fact must remain that in a simple environment, such as they had come from many, if not the majority, would have continued to live normal lives and never have become inmates of hospitals for the insane.

The fact that the artificial and stressing environment into which they are thrown in our large cities, whether at work or at home, either causes or stimulates the onset of mental disturbance, should entitle the foreign-born to further consideration than is often granted them. Stricter and more stringent examination before they embark and at the port of entry,[2] with a lessened zeal in deporting those who become insane while occupied in industries in the land of

[1] S. H. C., 30th A. R., p. 77.

[2] *The Evening Post*, New York, editorial, "A Better Immigration Service," Nov. 26, 1919.

their adoption, might be a saner and more humane policy to follow.[1]

XI. YEARS RESIDENT IN UNITED STATES

The figures indicating the distribution of the patients according to the years in the United States (Table 13) show very clearly the influence of the war in stopping immigration, for there were only 32 patients admitted who had come to this country within four years. There were 127 in the country from four to six years; 201 from eleven to fifteen years; 307 were native born.

TABLE 13. YEARS IN UNITED STATES

	Male.	Female.	Total.
Less than 1 year	2	2	4
1–3	18	10	28
4–6	79	48	127
7–10	99	73	172
11–15	111	90	201
Over 15	167	121	288
Life	197	110	307
Totals	673	454	1,127

With the end of the war, a new wave of immigration has begun, and efforts should be redoubled to keep out those who are either physically or mentally ill, or who are liable, because of constitutional weakness or inferiority, to break down under the stress and strain involved in the adjustment to a new environment and more exacting occupations.

XII. NEW IMMIGRATION LAW AND INSANITY

The new immigration law which passed both houses of Congress over the President's veto and became effective May

[1] Ward, Robert DeC., "The Crisis in our Immigration Policy," *The Institutional Quarterly*; official organ of the Public Charity Service of Illinois, vol. iv, no. ii, 1913, p. 14.

1, 1917, contains many provisions that will aid New York State in its efforts to free itself from the burden of the alien insane.

Section 3 provides for the exclusion of persons who have had one or more attacks of insanity at any time previously, instead of "persons who have been insane within five years previous;" and adds to the excluded classes persons of constitutional psychopathic inferiority and persons with chronic alcoholism.

The law further imposes a fine upon transportation companies of $200 for bringing in cases of insanity, constitutional psychopathic inferiority and chronic alcoholism. If "such mental or physical defect might have been detected by means of a competent medical examination," at the time of embarkation, an additional fine of $25 is imposed.

Section 11-a details "inspectors and matrons of the United States Immigration Service for duty on vessels carrying immigrant or emigrant passengers between foreign ports and ports of the United States." The object of this is to afford more thorough observation and examination of aliens, not only for the purpose of detecting diseases and mental and physical defects but to lighten the work of the medical inspectors at the port of entry.

The new law further provides that all aliens shall be examined by not less than two medical officers and two inspectors. This new method in a short while resulted in the rejection for mental defects of 9.27 per cent of the immigrants, whereas formerly only 2.29 per cent were thus rejected.

Furthermore, the new act authorizes the deportation of "any alien who, within five years after entry, becomes a public charge from causes not affirmatively shown to have arisen subsequent to landing." The time limit for deportation has been changed from 3 to 5 years and made retroactive.[1] Through the enforcement of these measures it is expected that a larger proportion of mentally sick and defective persons will be excluded than has heretofore been the case. The test of the efficacy of the machinery to be provided will come during the first few years following the resumption of the normal flow of immigrants.

XIII. DISPOSITION OF PATIENTS

The best, and in most of the states the only organized agency for dealing medically with mental disorders is the state hospital. Outside of the walls of such institutions the field of psychiatry is practically a neglected waste.[2] The result of this is that a striking contrast prevails between intra-hospital and extra-hospital knowledge and methods. The lack of knowledge of the hospitals and their work is very pronounced among the general public. As Table 14 indicates, of the total admissions numbering 1,127 patients, 790 or 70.9 per cent were committed to state hospitals. In nearly every case in which relatives were asked to sign commitment papers, with occasional exceptions when readmitted patients were involved, the question of the kind of institution the patient was being sent to, the probable duration of his stay there, the nature of the treatment, *etc.*, had to be fully explained before commitment papers were signed. The failure to be fairly well informed in such matters is due to many reasons and will be considered in another connection.

The several private institutions listed, namely, Rivercrest, Amityville, Dr. McFarland's, Belle Meade, Spring Hill, Green's Farms, and Dr. Combe's, received in all 24 male and 14 female patients, a total of 38 or 3.3 per cent of the

[1] S. H. C., 29th A. R., pp. 63-66.

[2] Russell, Wm. L., "What the State Hospitals can do in Mental Hygiene," *Mental Hygiene*, Jan., 1917, pp. 88-89.

TABLE 14. DISPOSITION OF PATIENTS

	Male.	Female.	Total.
Manhattan S. H.	252	201	453
Central Islip S. H.	184	147	331
Kings Park S. H.	4	2	6
Rivercrest Sanit.	17	8	25
Amityville Sanit.	1	1	2
Dr. McFarland's Sanit.	..	1	1
Belle Meade Sanit	4	1	5
Spring Hill Sanit.	1	..	1
Green's Farm Sanit.	1	..	1
Dr. Combe's Sanit.	..	3	3
Randall's Is.	4	1	5
Waverly House	..	2	2
House of Refuge	1	..	1
Inwood House	..	1	1
Dept. of Pub. Char.	6	2	8
Trans. to other Wards	9	2	11
Tomb's Prison	26	1	27
Returned to Court	10	5	15
Discharged	138	70	208
Died	13	6	19
Truant School	2	..	2
Totals	673	454	1,127

total admissions, or 4.5 per cent of the patients admitted to state institutions. The reason so few were committed to private sanatoria was because of the economic condition of the patients and their next of kin or friends; in fact, many of those sent to these institutions were withdrawn within a few weeks due to lack of funds and transferred to state hospitals.

The New York City Children's Hospital and School, an institution for mental defectives, received five patients: 2 morons, 1 low-grade moron, 2 imbeciles. These patients had became troublesome at home or were found on the streets by the police and brought to the psychopathic wards.

Waverly House, a temporary shelter for delinquent girls over 16 years of age, sent one young woman who had attempted suicide, for examination and disposition. She was diagnosed as being constitutionally inferior and returned to the shelter. One boy came from the House of Refuge, a custodial institution for delinquents; he was found to be constitutionally inferior, and was returned to the institution.

Inwood House, a custodial institution and reformatory home for wayward girls and women, sent one girl for examination because of what were thought to be symptoms of mental disorder. Examination showed that she was a mental defective (moron) afflicted with tertiary syphilis; she was returned to the institution whence she came.

The 2 boys returned to the truant school from which they had been sent for mental examination and observation were found to be morons.

The patients sent to the Department of Public Charities, (now the Department of Public Welfare) were transferred to the City Hospital, Blackwell's Island. Of the 2 females, 1 was an epileptic, the other a case of senility; among the 6 males, there were 2 cases of arteriosclerosis, 1 chronic alcoholic, 1 chronic nephritic, 1 of cerebral syphilis, 1 of cancer of the tongue. All of these showed some slight mental disturbance besides being chronic somatic cases; they were not however, considered suitable patients for a state hospital.

Such patients as were found to need further hospital treatment but were not suitable cases for the psychopathic wards were transferred to other wards of the hospital. This happened in the case of 11 patients, nearly all of whom were either alcoholics or drug addicts, or cases of attempted suicide detained as prisoners under Article 202, Section 2,303 of the Penal Law which provided that "every person guilty of attempting suicide is guilty of a felony, punishable by imprisonment in a state prison not exceeding two years, or by a fine not exceeding one thousand dollars, or both."

Upon being returned to the magistrate's courts after recovery, the patients who attempted suicide were as a rule lectured by the magistrate and discharged from custody. This section of the Penal Law, making an attempt at suicide a crime punishable by fine or imprisonment or both, was repealed May 5, 1919,[1] and there is no longer any legal restriction affecting suicidal attempts.

XIV. MENTAL EXAMINATION OF PRISONERS

Judges in the courts of the city sent 27 persons to the psychopathic wards for mental examination, after having first remanded them to the City Prison (The Tombs) to await indictment and trial; in several instances lawyers requested that their clients be sent to the hospital for mental examination in order to determine the mental responsibility of the prisoners, often hoping thereby to obtain either a reduced or suspended sentence, or to have the prisoners paroled, if guilty of the indictment. The following table indicates the diagnoses in these cases:

TABLE 15. DIAGNOSIS OF PRISONERS

	Male.	Female.
Constitutionally Inferior	9	
Mental Def. (Moron)	7	1
Mental Def. (Imbecile)	1	
* Dementia Praecox	3	
Psychoneurosis	1	
Chronic Heroin User	1	
Manic Depressive, Mixed	1	
Chorea	1	
Not Insane	2	
Totals	26	1

* Two were former patients in state hospitals; one came from another state.

[1] *Laws* of 1919, chap. 414.

Better and more adequate facilities for the mental examination of adult prisoners, as is already provided in the children's courts,[1] would help guide magistrates and judges in intelligently disposing of the cases of those appearing before them in whom some mental abnormality exists.[2] There were in addition 10 males and 5 females sent for examination directly from the courts and upon examination 4 were found to be mental defectives (morons); 2 constitutionally inferior; 1 psychoneurotic; 4 who were cases of attempted suicide, were diagnosed as not insane; and 3 were found to be of normal mental make-up.

XV. MENTAL DEFICIENCY LAW

To meet the problem of providing proper custodial care for mental defectives and of otherwise looking after the welfare both of the community and of the mental defectives therein, Chapter 633, Laws of 1919, was passed and became a law on May 14, 1919. This act, known as the Mental Deficiency Law, provides for the appointment of a Commission of Mental Defectives, of which Dr. Pearce Bailey has since been appointed chairman. Among other things, provision is made in Section 24-a for the diagnosis and treatment for mentally defective persons before or after trial. This section of the law reads as follows:

> Any person alleged to be mentally defective . . . arraigned on a criminal charge may be committed before or after trial or conviction to a hospital or other suitable place selected by the state commission for mental defectives . . . for a period not to exceed ten days, for examination as to his mental and physical condition, by any court or magistrate. . . . If the examination discloses that the alleged mentally defective person

[1] Baldwin and Flexner, *op. cit.*, p. 127.

[2] *Vide* studies of prisoners in psychiatric clinic of Sing Sing, by Bernard Glueck, *Mental Hygiene*, Jan., 1918, pp. 85-151; *Mental Hygiene*, April, 1918, pp. 177-218.

is of such a nature as to require his supervision, control and care for his own welfare or for his own welfare and the welfare of others or for the welfare of the community, the judge or justice shall issue an order for his commitment to one of the state institutions for mental defectives.

The Commission has designated Bellevue Hospital, Manhattan, and Kings County and the Cumberland Street Hospitals, Brooklyn, as the institutions in New York City to which such cases shall be sent.

XVI. DISCHARGES FROM PSYCHOPATHIC WARDS

The crowded conditions in the psychopathic wards as well as in the state hospitals are sufficient to induce physicians in the psychopathic wards to permit relatives who refuse to sign papers for the commitment of mild and borderline cases to take such patients home after contracting to be responsible for any damage or injury they may cause. This has led to the discharge of a number of such patients to the custody of friends and relatives. Almost invariably, with the possible exceptions where patients are taken out of the city or are sent to private sanatoria, the relatives of such discharged patients return within a short time stating that due to their inability properly to care and provide for the patients taken home against the advice of the doctors, they are prepared to have such patients committed to state hospitals. Table 16 lists the discharges according to diagnosis; there were 138 males and 70 females, a total of 208, equivalent to 18.4 per cent of the total number of admissions.

It is almost needless to remark that were there in New York an institution to which a number of the above patients might have been sent, as to a psychopathic hospital, relatives would consider a stay in such an institution advisable and would not have taken the mentally ailing back to their poor and uninviting homes, only to have a more

TABLE 16. DIAGNOSIS OF DISCHARGES

	Male.	Female.	Totals.
Senile Psychosis	8	1	9
Arteriosclerosis	4	..	4
Organic Nervous Disease	4	2	6
General Paralysis	13	..	13
Cerebral Lues	2	..	2
Brain Tumor	1	..	1
Cerebral Hemorrhage	1	..	1
Alcoholism	12	2	14
Heroin Poisoning	1	8	9
Infection Exhaustion Psych.	..	5	5
Manic Depressive	19	15	34
Dementia Praecox	27	9	36
Paranoid Condition	6	1	7
Epilepsy	13	3	16
Psychoneurosis	3	..	3
Hysterical Episode	1	7	8
Constitutionally Inferior	1	5	6
Mental Defective	7	4	11
Depression Undifferentiated	1	4	5
Transitory Confusion	5	2	7
Unclassified	5	..	5
Not Insane	4	2	6
Totals	138	70	208

serious relapse within a short time, with commitment to a state hospital the only alternative.

XVII. DEATHS IN PSYCHOPATHIC WARDS

Nineteen patients died in the psychopathic wards, 13 males and 6 females. A number of these had been transferred from other wards in the hospital in which they had become unmanageable and a disturbance to the other patients in the wards with them.

Table 17 indicates the cause of death:

TABLE 17. DIAGNOSIS OF DEATHS

	Male.	Female.	Totals.
Pneumonia	4	3	7
Infection Exhaustion	1	1	2
General Paralysis	2	..	2
Pulmonary Tuberculosis	2	..	2
Brain Tumor	2	..	2
Tubercular Meningitis	1	..	1
Pleurisy	1	..	1
Blood Poisoning	..	1	1
Cerebral Spinal Lues	..	1	1
Totals	13	6	19

XVIII. SUMMARY

In this chapter the aim has been not merely to present the statistics dealing with the psychopathic ward admissions, but also thereby to indicate the many needs that must be met ere a more effective policy in dealing with mental cases in New York City and State can be evolved. The problem is not a simple one nor easy of solution, as the mere difficulty in obtaining or agreeing upon an adequate and satisfactory definition as to what constitutes mental alienation or insanity has shown. Psychiatry is of recent origin and the human ills it aims to help and to cure are manifold. Still, with the information already at hand, and the augmentation thereof that we may look forward to, it is not too much to ask nor yet to expect that those who are in the service of the state in this particular field shall assist the community not only to return those of unsound mind to a condition of sanity, but shall also take the lead in educating the public to a fuller understanding of the causes, preventatives and cures of insanity, as far as available scientific knowledge will permit.

CHAPTER III

RESULTS OF STATE HOSPITAL CARE AND TREATMENT

I. NEED AND PROVISIONS FOR SCIENTIFIC STUDY OF INSANITY

Scientific observation and experience form the firm foundation upon which the whole question of the care of the insane is based. Every step forward—and many steps backward—in the care of the insane are more or less closely related with the medical conceptions regarding the existence and the causes of insanity. It has become more and more the duty of the state to foster scientific investigations in the hospitals for the insane. In this respect psychiatry has long enough been treated as a stepchild. Although our old asylum physicians afford brilliant examples of what can be accomplished with very inadequate means in the attainment of high scientific ideals, the state has only recently recognized that a healthful progress in the care of the insane is not possible without a continuous development of scientific work.[1]

Thus wrote Kraepelin of the development of experimental and laboratory work and research in his native country, and his words may very properly be applied to conditions as they have existed and still exist with but few exceptions, in the United States. To meet just this problem as well as to centralize research aiming to achieve a better understanding and knowledge of the etiology of the various forms of insanity, and likewise to discover cures therefor, the State Hospital Commission (at that time the State Commission in

[1]Quoted by Drewry, Wm. F., "Care and Condition of the Insane in Virginia," *Nat'l. Conf. of Char. and Corr. Report*, 1908, p. 307.

Lunacy) in 1896 organized the Pathological Institute, now known as the Psychiatric Institute. This agency through its medical officers acts as the standardizing factor in the state hospital system, instructing the physicians in the several hospitals in the application of a standard classification of the psychoses, in the organization of the clinical or out-patient service as well as of the staff meetings, in the work of the pathological laboratory, and also in the compilation of the medical statistics.[1] Though all of this work is important, the institute is greatly hampered because of the lack of a sufficiently large appropriation with which to carry on necessary and extensive investigations, the allotment to this division of the state hospital system for the year 1918 having been only about $28,000,[2] a smaller amount than was appropriated for this work twenty years ago.[3]

One of the prime necessities for scientific research in the field of mental diseases is a sufficiently large and varied number of patients, presenting many forms of mental alienation, together with a wide range in social status, environment, occupation, nationality, *etc.* In the New York State Hospitals for the insane there were under treatment on June 30, 1918, 33,868 patients supported wholly by the state, 3,303 reimbursing patients, and 181 private cases, making a total of 37,352,[4] probably the largest number of patients under institutional care in any state in the country. Since the thirteen civil state hospitals are located in different

[1] S. H. C., 30th A. R., 1918, p. 144.

[2] *Ibid.*, p. 267.

[3] *Ibid.*, p. 267. The largest amount appropriated was in 1899, when $36,000 was granted; the largest amount spent was in 1897, $40,058.28. Since then the appropriations as well as the expenditures have been between $20,000 and $30,000 per annum, except in 1900, when $35,155.53 was spent, though only $20,000 was originally appropriated.

[4] S. H. C., 30th A. R., p. 327.

parts of the state, each receiving patients from the district in which it is situated, there is sufficient laboratory material upon which to draw for scientific purposes. Insofar as the factor of different nationalities represented among the patients is concerned, it might be interesting to note that there were almost forty countries which contributed to the insane population of the New York hospitals, though the native-born in these hospitals for the year ending June 30, 1918 were over half of the total, namely 55.5 per cent.[1] Considering this wealth of clinical and pathological material, as well as the large number of specialists engaged in the care and treatment of these 37,352 patients, it would seem that much information of a helpful and serviceable nature in effecting recoveries of insane persons should be forthcoming from those associated in the psychiatric, psychologic and pathologic work in the New York State Hospitals.

These institutions, rated among the best of their kind in America, have not, however, witnessed the issuance from within their walls of contributions of unusual worth in the field of psychiatry, nor in the other branches, namely, psychology or pathology. This failure has not been altogether, if at all, the fault of the psychiatrists and others who should rightfully have been expected to carry on researches of particular scientific importance. It has rather been due, as pointed out above, to the failure on the part of the state to appropriate sufficient money for the work of the psychiatric institute, and furthermore, to still another factor—the overcrowding which has existed in the state hospitals for many years, with the concomitant shortage of physicians, nurses, laboratory technicians, attendants, *etc.* It is to this latter problem in particular that practically all hospital superintendents have had to devote much of their time, for

[1] S. H. C., 30th A. R., p. 292.

with little extension of building operations during the past few years and with an ever increasing population and a proportionate increase in the number of cases of insanity committed to the already overcrowded state hospitals, the problem has become more aggravated each year.[1]

II. OVERCROWDING

The following table indicates the overcrowding of the state hospitals as conditions existed on June 30, 1918.[2]

TABLE 18. OVERCROWDING IN THE STATE HOSPITALS

Hospitals.	Population June 30, 1918, Excluding Paroles.	Rated Capacity.	Overcrowding.	
			No.	Per cent.
Binghamton	2,701	2,400	301	12.5
Brooklyn	884	637	247	38.8
Buffalo	2,202	1,700	502	29.5
Central Islip	5,040	4,100	940	22.9
Gowanda	1,281	950	331	34.8
Hudson River	3,428	2,850	578	20.3
Kings Park	4,479	3,500	979	28.0
Manhattan	5,327	4,250	1,077	25.3
Middletown	2,181	1,800	381	21.2
Rochester	1,541	1,260	281	22.3
St. Lawrence	2,285	1,950	335	17.2
Utica	1,687	1,400	287	20.5
Willard	2,426	2,200	226	10.3
Totals	35,462	28,997	6,465	22.3

There appears but little possibility of lessening the over-

[1] Page, Charles Whitney, *The Care of the Insane and Hospital Management*, 1912; presents a discussion of the method to be followed in choosing a superintendent, his qualifications, duties, his official relation to officers and employees, etc.

[2] S. H. C., 30th A. R., p. 235. Also Hastings, George A., "Some Essentials of a State Program for Mental Hygiene," *State Char. Aid Assn. Publication*, no. 146, pp. 11-14.

crowded conditions before plans thus far developed by the Hospital Development Commission are carried out.[1] Among the more important recommendations of the commission are: A new state hospital at Creedmoor; enlarging the hospitals in and near New York City; securing a site for a new hospital in the metropolitan district in place of the abandoned Mohansic institution; the establishment of a psychopathic hospital in New York City; completion of a state hospital at Marcy near Utica; a more orderly method of making appropriations; better planning of institutions, and more preventive and research work.[2]

III. EXTENSION OF OBSERVATION PERIOD

Still another factor in the overcrowding of the state hospitals has been the shortness of the detention period in the observation wards of the municipal institutions. Patients brought to the psychopathic wards of Bellevue and other hospitals are not kept there for a sufficient length of time to permit those suffering from slight attacks to recover prior to their commitment to a state hospital.[3] The reasons for this are two-fold; in the first place, the officers of the observation or psychopathic wards, particularly of the largest among them, Bellevue, to which came the cases considered in this work, have for a number of years been facing the same difficulty as the state hospitals, to wit, lack of sufficient accommodations. Were it possible to detain a number of the so-called hopeful cases for ten days or more until they had recovered from the attack which caused them to be

[1] *Survey*, Jan. 26, 1918, p. 467, "Crowding in the Insane Hospitals."

[2] S. H. C., 30th A. R., pp. 235-236.

[3] Mason, Frank H., "Modern Hospital for the Insane," *Daily Consular Reports, Dept. of Commerce and Labor*, no. 2264, May 22, 1905; gives an illustrated description of the reception hospital erected by the city of Munich, Germany, for the temporary care and treatment of incipient cases. Dr. Emil Kraepelin was appointed director of this hospital.

brought to the psychopathic ward, in the majority of such cases commitment to a state hospital might have been avoided. It is quite apparent that such a plan would in practice amount to a working out of the psychopathic hospital idea within the limited confines of wards in municipal hospitals. Any means employed to decrease the crowded conditions of our state hospitals and at the same time aid in the early recovery of a number of patients would be welcomed by all interested in the proper care and treatment of the insane. The second reason for the short duration of the observation period lies in that provision of the Insanity Law which reads as follows: "In no case shall any insane person be confined in any other place than a state hospital or duly licensed institution for the insane, for a period longer than ten days."[1] This of course makes it impossible for any municipal hospital maintaining a psychopathic service to detain an insane or alleged insane person longer than the period of time prescribed in the law, though an extension of this period, if limited to cases indicated, would undoubtedly result in much benefit.

Table 19 indicates that 47, or about 6 per cent of the patients were transferred to state hospitals within 24 hours after their arrival in Bellevue Hospital. It should be pointed out, however, that most of these were cases that were out on parole from one of the state hospitals and had been brought to the psychopathic wards of Bellevue Hospital for transfer to the institution from which they had been paroled. Among the others were a number whose parole period had expired and who had suffered a recurrent attack, necessitating their re-commitment to the state hospital, usually to the one in which they had been previously confined. There were 172 who were transferred within two days, 192 in three days, 129 in four days, giving a total

[1] Chap. 27 of the Consolidated Laws, "The Insanity Law," sec. 87.

TABLE 19. NUMBER OF DAYS SPENT IN PSYCHOPATHIC WARDS OF BELLEVUE HOSPITAL PRIOR TO COMMITMENT TO STATE HOSPITAL

No. of Days.	Manhattan.		Central Is.		Kings Park.		Totals.
	Male.	Female.	Male.	Female.	Male.	Female.	Male and Female.
1	8	10	20	5	4	..	47
2	48	39	38	47	..	..	172
3	56	55	41	39	..	1	192
4	43	35	27	23	..	1	129
5	29	25	20	9	..	..	83
6	22	8	15	8	..	..	53
7	13	8	6	5	..	..	32
8	11	8	6	4	..	..	29
9	4	2	5	1	..	..	12
10	12	6	4	4	..	..	26
Over 10	6	5	2	2	..	..	15
Totals	252	201	184	147	4	2	790

of 540 or 68.3 per cent transferred within four days from the time of admission; 83 were detained five days, making the percentage 78.8 per cent of the total kept in the psychopathic wards less than one-half the maximum time allowed by law. Most of the 15 who were kept in the psychopathic wards over ten days were remanded to the hospital by some court for observation and examination, and the ensuing complications resulted in their detention one or more days beyond the ten-day period; the few remaining cases could not be transferred to a state hospital within ten days because of their mental or physical condition, or both.

Dr. Henry Maudsley was among the first to propose the erection of an observation hospital for the treatment of incipient mental cases in London. The purposes of this hospital were to be largely those assigned to psychopathic hospitals at the present time. In smaller communities, however, where institutions of large size are unnecessary, psychopathic wards in the local general hospitals would often be the means of preventing insanity and accomplishing the early recovery of incipient cases, provided, of course, that the law was changed to allow a longer detention period than is at present prescribed.

Among the states making specific mention in their laws of the length of time patients may be kept in observation or psychopathic wards, California provides that the board of supervisors of each city or county must maintain a room or rooms suitable for the detention, care and treatment of alleged insane persons, for a period of not more than twenty days.[1] The District of Columbia permits the detention of such persons in the government hospital for the insane or in any other hospital for a period not exceeding thirty days.[2] Michigan allows for the detention in any hospital, home or retreat for not more than thirty days, except by special order of the court.[3] In the State of Pennsylvania, persons suffering from mental disorders may be committed for not more than thirty days to the psychopathic wards of hospitals for observation and treatment in the same manner as persons are committed to hospitals for the insane; but persons admitted to these wards who are found insane must be regularly committed and removed to a hospital for the insane within thirty days.[4] Some of the more important advantages of such an extended period over the ten days allowed by law in New York State, may be summed up as follows:[5]

[1] *Political Code of California*, 1905, as amended by *Laws* of 1909, chap. 65, sec. 2167.

[2] *Revised Statutes of the United States, Act of 1904*, 33 Stat. 316.

[3] *Laws* of 1909, pp. 16, 185.

[4] *Laws* of 1911, chap. 855, sec. 2.

[5] Briggs, L. Vernon, "What can be done for the Prevention of Insanity by the Treatment of Incipient Cases in General Hospitals," *Amer. Jo. of Ins.*, April, 1911, p. 660.

1. The incipient case would have the advantage of immediate expert care by members of the hospital staff in every branch of medicine and surgery.

2. He would have the advantage of a large hospital nursing staff instead of attendants.

3. The social considerations after recovery are most important to patients, many of whom would thus be saved from being placed in an insane asylum.

IV. PRIVATE SANATORIA AND HOSPITALS

There were in the State of New York in 1918 a total of twenty-four private licensed institutions[1] with a licensed capacity of 1,522 patients. It is these asylums or retreats which serve the purpose of wards in general hospitals, but they are only within the reach of those whose relatives or friends are in a position to pay from $25.00 to $100.00 or more a week. Many incipient cases are discharged as recovered or improved within a few weeks from these private institutions, in which they have been given much individual attention, more than could possibly be accorded them in the state hospitals. This does not of course mean that the state hospitals are failing to effect cures, but rather that for incipient cases some institutions other than state hospitals are at present prepared to render better service, and hence increase the ratio of recoveries, because of proportionately larger staffs, better equipment, and less overcrowding. The psychopathic wards or "Pavilion F" of the Albany Hospital are rendering a service that many of the similar institutions throughout the state should be prepared and equipped to give.[2] This is a private institution maintained for charitable purposes and those treated there are required

[1] "The Insanity Law," art. 3, sec. 59.

[2] Mosher, J. M., "The Treatment of Mental Disease in a General Hospital," *The Modern Hospital*, Nov., 1915.

to pay or to be paid for by relatives or friends, if they possess the means; the charges include the usual and rather moderate amounts asked for the care of the patients and for the payment of private nurses, if such are found to be necessary.[1] The development of psychopathic hospitals in the large cities, of psychopathic wards in general hospitals in the smaller cities of the state, and an extension of the ten-day detention period, would prove to be important elements in the reduction of the number of committed cases, in lessening the overcrowding of the state hospitals, and in markedly increasing the early recovery of incipient cases of mental disorder.

V. CLASSIFICATION OF PATIENTS AT STATE HOSPITALS

In the preceding chapter it was pointed out that of those admitted to the psychopathic wards of Bellevue Hospital during one year, the following number of patients were committed to state hospitals:

	Male.	Female.	Totals.
To Manhattan State Hosp...	252	201	453
To Central Islip S. H........	184	147	331
To Kings Park S. H........	4	2	6
Totals	440	350	790

Upon arriving at the state hospitals, the patients are as a rule sent to the reception wards or buildings, in which they are detained until properly diagnosed and classified. The superintendents of state hospitals have for a long time made

[1] Mosher, "Need of Early Treatment for Mental Diseases," *Amer. Jo. of Ins.*, Jan., 1909, pp. 501-503; Drury, William F., *Evolution of Psychiatry*, 1904, p. 42.

efforts to promote and carry out a greater uniformity in classification according to age, nationality, education, station in life and diagnosis of those assigned to particular wards.[1] However, the overcrowding in all the hospitals, the large wards and the insufficiency of the staffs have made it well-nigh impossible to carry out these plans, except insofar as relates to placing patients in wards according to diagnosis, behavior, and the acuteness or chronicity of the ailment. In planning one of the large state hospitals in New York some years ago, the medical superintendent submitted plans which called for a number of cottages, each with a capacity of twenty-five patients, the purpose in mind being to permit the classification of the patients along the lines outlined above. When the total outlay for erecting and maintaining such a cottage system was estimated, the amount necessary was found to be far greater than the state had appropriated for the new institution and intended to allow for maintenance and upkeep from year to year. The result was that instead of erecting separate cottages with accommodations for not more than thirty patients, buildings housing from 125 to 150 patients were erected, with less satisfactory provisions for the separation and classification of the different groups in the hospital population.

VI. OCCUPATIONAL THERAPY AT STATE HOSPITALS

After the assignment of patients to their wards, an attempt is made to give them some form of occupation suitable to their particular needs and requirements. Several classes for the reeducation of the patients are maintained in most of the hospitals, though the total number of patients benefiting from such instruction is small. Thus, in 1918, in the Manhattan State Hospital, with about 5,500 patients in the wards, there were only 150 who received instruction

[1] *State Hospital Quarterly*, Aug., 1919, p. 439.

in the arts and crafts classes.[1] In a survey made of the Manhattan State Hospital by the New York State Department of Efficiency and Economy, it was reported that the institution obtained excellent production from the land under cultivation, as well as from the hospital industries. This statement in itself is not sufficient evidence of the efficiency of industrial departments in the hospital, for it fails to take into consideration the number or percentage of inmates employed in these industries, even though it seemingly makes allowance for the high per capita production. Mention is made of the fact that of 245 arable acres only 66 acres were under cultivation at the time the study was made.[2]

The possibility of providing occupational therapy for a larger percentage of the patients under treatment is indicated by the experiences of the Bloomingdale Hospital at White Plains, where, with a total of 437 patients in 1918, there was a daily average attendance of 97 patients in the departments of occupational therapy, in which a large variety of occupations are taught.[3] The marked difference between conditions at the Manhattan State Hospital and the Bloomingdale asylum is due to a number of reasons, among them being the difficulty experienced in trying to educate certain types of mental cases, of which larger numbers are to be found in the state institutions than at Bloomingdale, which proportionately treats a larger number of cases of manic depressive insanity, and a smaller number of cases of senility, general paralysis, and dementia praecox; the lack of a sufficient number of properly trained sup-

[1] S. H. C., 30th A. R., p. 201.

[2] McCalmut, M. E., *Report of the New York State Dept. of Efficiency and Economy*, "Organization and Administration of New York State Hospitals for the Insane," 1915, p. 418.

[3] *Annual Report*, Society of the New York Hospital, 1918, pp. 11-12.

ervisors and teachers of trades; the failure of the state hospitals to develop a definite policy regarding the training and education of the patients, and also the large number and variety of trades and occupations represented among the patients in the state institutions. Considering only the 790 patients dealt with in this work, the diversity of employment prior to admission to the state hospitals is evident from the following tables:

TABLE 20. OCCUPATIONS OF MALES

Occupation	Number	Occupation	Number
Actor	1	Factory hand	3
Agent	4	Farmer	1
Artist	1	Florist	1
Auctioneer	1	Furniture maker	1
Author	1	Furrier	2
Baker	2	Gasfitter	1
Barber	2	Grocer	2
Bartender	1	Hairworker	1
Bookbinder	2	Harnessmaker	1
Bookkeeper	8	Hatmaker	1
Brass worker	2	Helper	1
Brushmaker	1	Insurance agent	1
Butcher	3	Interpreter	1
Button hole maker	1	Ironworker	3
Buttonmaker	1	Janitor	1
Canvasser	1	Jeweler	2
Capmaker	3	Junk dealer	2
Caretaker	1	Laborer	37
Carpenter	3	Laundry worker	1
Chauffeur	2	Letter carrier	1
Chemist	1	Longshoreman	2
Cigar maker	7	Lunchman	1
Clerk	42	Machinist	6
Cutter	9	Manager	1
Deck hand	1	Manufacturer	1
Designer	1	Mechanic	2
Dishwasher	1	Mechanical dentist	2
Draughtsman	1	Messenger	11
Driver	5	Motorman	1
Electrician	4	Musician	2
Embroiderer	2	Newspaper illustrator	1
Engineer R. R.	1	Operator	26

Occupation	Number	Occupation	Number
Packer	4	Stenographer	1
Painter	9	Storekeeper	1
Paper-box maker	4	Student	3
Paper roller	1	Street car conductor	1
Peddler	17	Suspendermaker	1
Photographer	3	Tailor	35
Pipemaker	1	Teacher	3
Plumber	1	Telegraph operator	1
Pocketbook maker	1	Telephone operator	1
Porter	1	Ticket speculator	1
Presser	9	Tinsmith	3
Printer	11	Truckman	1
Salesman	32	Upholsterer	3
School pupil	7	Watchmaker	2
Sheet metal maker	2	Waiter	7
Shoemaker	4	Window cleaner	3
Singer	1	No occupation	22
Soda dispenser	1		
Soldier	6	Totals	440
Special officer	1		

TABLE 21. OCCUPATIONS OF FEMALES

Occupation	Number	Occupation	Number
Artificial flower maker	1	Milliner	5
Bookbinder	1	Model	1
Bookkeeper	5	Musician	2
Capmaker	1	Neckwear	2
Cashier	1	Needlework	1
Cigar-box maker	1	Operator	29
Clerk	7	Paper box maker	4
Clothes cleaner	1	Peddler	1
Doll maker	1	Pocketbook maker	1
Domestic	8	Salesgirl	2
Dressmaker	11	School pupil	8
Envelope maker	1	Seamstress	2
Errand girl	1	Stenographer	13
Factory hand	4	Teacher, music	3
Glove maker	1	Waist examiner	4
Housework	185	Waitress	1
Interpreter	1	Watchmaker	1
Jewelry dealer	1	No occupation	35
Laundress	2		
Leather goods worker	1	Totals	350

The above tables indicating the list of occupations of both

males and females show that it would be impossible as well as impracticable to establish industries within the hospital walls and grounds akin to those in which the patients were engaged prior to commitment. It is quite apparent from a perusal of these lists that there are many trades and occupations which are not listed here, simply because among the patients considered certain industrial and commercial activities are not as common as among other people. Thus, among the males, there is to be found but a small number of patients who were employed in the building and mechanical lines, whereas there is a comparatively large number represented among the clerks, salesmen, tailors, clothing operators, and kindred or allied trades. The same difference is also found among the females. There were only eight domestics, though a considerable number of the single young women were foreign born, and a large number in the needle trades. The 185 patients indicated as being engaged in housework represent married women caring for their own households, not leaving their homes to become domestics or servants in the homes of others.

The intent and purpose of the discussion of the trades and occupations of the patients will become more apparent in the last chapter of this work, for there thought will be given to ways and means of providing gainful occupation for discharged and paroled patients, as well as for those who may under unfavorable circumstances and conditions become so ill mentally as to make their commitment to a state hospital advisable. As pointed out above, the aim has also been to indicate the inadequacy of present accommodations and provisions in the state hospitals for the therapeutic treatment of patients through a sufficiently varied and interesting scheme of light occupations.

VII. READMISSIONS TO STATE HOSPITALS

One very important way properly to gauge the efficacy of the care and treatment accorded patients in state hospitals is to consider the proportion of patients that find it necessary to return to the hospitals from which they have been discharged or paroled, or taken home by relatives. There are necessarily a number of factors that enter into such a consideration, among them being the over-crowding in the hospitals, the ratio of officers, nurses, and attendants to the number of patients, diagnoses of the patients permitted to leave the hospital, and ease with which patients may be returned to the institutions. Of the 8,700 total admissions to the state hospitals for the year 1918, 6,797 or 78.1 per cent were first admissions; 1,903, or 21.9 per cent were readmissions.[1] There was a marked difference between the readmission rates among the several hospitals; the Brooklyn State Hospital had a readmission percentage of only 16.7, largely because of the disproportionate number of senile cases quartered there, whereas there was a percentage of 28.4 of readmissions in the Middletown State Hospital.[2] The readmission rates for the two hospitals which figure largely in this study, namely Manhattan and Central Islip State Hospitals, were 18.9 per cent for the former, and 21.4 per cent for the latter. Table 22 indicates the readmissions to the state hospitals of the Jewish patients, who were admitted to these institutions from Bellevue Hospital during the year beginning September 1, 1917 and ending August 31, 1918:

[1] S. H. C., 30th A. R., p. 278.

[2] *Ibid.*, p. 343.

TABLE 22. NUMBER OF READMISSIONS TO STATE HOSPITALS

No. of Admissions.	Central Islip.		Manhattan.		Kings Park.		Totals.	
	Male.	Female.	Male.	Female.	Male.	Female.	Male.	Female.
1	106	99	180	127	..	..	286	226
2	61	33	58	60	4	2	123	95
3	13	10	13	9	..	..	26	19
4	4	5	1	2	..	..	5	7
6	..	..	..	1	..	..	..	1
7	..	..	..	1	..	..	..	1
12	..	..	..	1	..	..	..	1
Totals	184	147	252	201	4	2	440	350

There were 512 first admissions and 278 readmissions to the three state hospitals to which the patients were committed, showing a readmission rate of 35.2 per cent for the Jewish cases sent to these institutions from Bellevue Hospital. This percentage is considerably higher than the rate for the entire state hospital system, and also higher than the rate of readmissioins to the Manhattan and Central Islip State Hospitals. In view of these facts, it might be advisable to consider in brief the elements that possibly contributed to this greater percentage of readmissions among the group studied in this work.

Several reasons have already been assigned for the return of patients to hospitals after they have once been discharged either as recovered or in an improved condition. There are, however, more specific and definite factors that can be held responsible for the high rate of readmissions that have been shown to be prevalent among the Jewish patients admitted to the state hospitals. It has been contended by some students of the subject that the cause of the larger proportion of readmissions among Jewish patients could be assigned almost entirely to the disproportionate number of certain of the psychoses appearing among these patients, particularly dementia praecox in all its variations, and also the several forms of manic depressive insanity.[1]

(a) *High Readmission Rates Among Jewish Patients.* In order to find what is probably the cardinal reason for the high readmission rates among the Jewish patients, it will again be necessary to revert to the figures for the state hospitals so as to have a basis upon which to make an accurate comparison. For the state as a whole, the per cent distribution among readmissions for the year 1918 was as follows: for dementia praecox the rate for the entire state was 31.2 per cent, with rates of 37.3 per cent for Manhattan State Hospital, and 35.0 per cent for Central Islip State Hospital; for manic depressive readmissions the rate was 36.5 per cent for the state as a whole, 36.6 per cent for Manhattan State Hospital and 33.1 per cent for Central Islip State Hospital.[2] From the percentages presented in Table 23 it is seen that the Jewish patients contributed, in fact, a smaller percentage of readmissions of cases of dementia praecox than either the state as a whole or Manhattan and Central Islip State Hospitals, while they seemingly were responsible for a higher readmission rate among the cases of manic depressive insanity than that which prevailed throughout the state, or in Manhattan and Central Islip State Hospitals. In reference to the latter group, the rate of readmissions to the Manhattan State Hospital for the preceding year, namely 1917, was likewise 41.8 per cent, identical with the rate of Jewish readmissions for the year 1918. Table 23 indicates the percentages in summarized form:

[1] S. H. C., 30th A. R., p. 376, for discussion of readmissions to all state hospitals.

[2] *Ibid.*, p. 294.

TABLE 23. DISTRIBUTION OF CERTAIN PSYCHOSES AMONG READMISSIONS

	Dementia Praecox.	Manic Depressive Insanity.
All State Hospitals	31.2	36.5
Manhattan State Hosp	37.3	36.6
Central Islip S. H	35.0	33.1
Jewish cases	30.5	41.8

Judging from the facts and figures presented above, it is seen that the high rate of readmissions among the Jewish patients as compared with the rate of readmissions to all the state hospitals cannot be ascribed to a higher rate of readmissions among the cases diagnosed as suffering from either dementia praecox or manic depressive insanity. The variation in the percentages of certain psychoses, particularly dementia praecox and manic depressive insanity, as shown in the statistics for all the state hospitals for a five year period indicate such a wide divergence,[1] that the only safe method that may be pursued in arriving at comparative figures is to take only the percentages for the hospitals to which the Jewish patients were admitted in large numbers. Following along these lines, the readmission rates to the Manhattan and Central Islip State Hospitals, as shown in Table 23, should be those which alone might properly be used to arrive at a just comparison. Even then, the Jewish patients as already explained, show up favorably when compared with the total readmissions, though they have a higher readmission rate among the cases of manic depressive insanity. The variation in the basis for diagnosis among the different hospitals, the marked difference between the reported percentages of certain of the psychoses among the several hospitals, despite the attempts of the staff of the

[1] S. H. C., 30th A. R., p. 294.

Psychiatric Institute to standardize the methods used in arriving at diagnoses for particular groups of cases, indicate that the statistics as thus far presented cannot be taken at full face value, at least insofar as the diagnoses of a large number of cases which may be classified as borderline are concerned.

VIII. REASONS FOR HIGH READMISSION RATES

The reasons for the higher rate of readmissions among the Jewish patients than among the others committed to the state hospitals are as yet unexplained, though a higher rate of readmissions among those patients diagnosed otherwise than dementia praecox and manic depressive insanity, may in part cover the added percentage of these readmissions. The importance of the question of a higher rate of readmissions among Jews involves even more fundamental matters than that of distribution of patients according to diagnosis. It again raises the question discussed in another connection, namely, the effect of a proper classification of patients according to social, racial, language, *etc.*, groups, upon the percentage of recoveries.

An indication of some of these difficulties encountered by the staff of workers in the wards is the statement recently made to the writer by a physician in one of the largest state hospitals. He remarked that he had in one of his wards a group of fifty patients whose language was entirely alien to him as well as to the nurses and attendants on the ward. The result was that these patients did not receive the attention that should have been bestowed upon them by the doctor and others in helping them to improve and ultimately to recover. This condition is particularly applicable to the Jewish patients of foreign birth, though the hospital authorities have tried to do all they could to remove such hindrances to the well-being and recovery of the large number of non-English speaking charges under their care. The question of agreeable and palatable food is a matter which applies particularly to Jewish patients, most of whom have been brought up in homes where the Jewish dietary laws are observed, for the eating of food that is not prepared according to these laws is more or less obnoxious. The result is that patients who understand the difference, among them being a large number of those ultimately paroled or discharged, demand of their relatives that steps be taken leading to their release from custody, often before they are sufficiently recovered to insure against a relapse. In the long run such premature discharges necessitate readmission to the hospital.

Assuming that the reasons for the high readmission rates among the Jewish patients can be ascribed to the causes just outlined, as well as to the fairly large number of cases of manic depressive insanity that have to be returned to the hospitals, the thought comes to mind that there must be some way or ways of so altering the present methods of dealing with the insane cared for in state institutions, that high readmission rates may be materially reduced. Several methods are obvious from the discussion of the subject, such as introducing into the hospitals physicians and nurses as well as attendants who understand the languages spoken by large groups of patients of foreign birth; applying a more thorough and selective classification to all the patients, supplying "kosher" kitchens in the hospitals in which large numbers of Jewish patients are cared for, *etc.* The impossibility of doing these several things at the present time because of the overcrowded conditions in the hospitals has already been touched upon, and nothing can be done along these lines until plans already prepared for the further extension of the facilities of the state hospitals are sufficiently matured to furnish a basis for further suggestion and criticism.

IX. MOVEMENTS FOR ESTABLISHMENT OF JEWISH PSYCHOPATHIC HOSPITALS

Referring particularly to Jewish patients, movements have been set afoot in New York City aiming at the establishment of a hospital for the mentally sick Jews whose diagnosis indicates a prognosis of possible recovery or at least of improvement so marked in both physical and mental conditions, as to render it advisable to care for and treat such patients in an institution resembling in plan and scope the psychopathic hospitals of Boston and Baltimore. Many members of the Jewish community in New York who have given this matter thought seem to agree that such an institution would not only be of much service to those unfortunates among the Jews who become mentally unbalanced, but would at the same time effect a higher proportion of cures, reduce the expenditure of state money, and also act as an experimental station for the study of various phases of the problem. The plans for such a hospital have not as yet progressed sufficiently to make it advisable to pass judgment upon the matter. However, it is safe to state that any project is worthy when its purpose is to reduce human suffering which is involved in the loss of the power to reason and to live the life of a rational being. Mental hygiene agencies have been at work in New York City as well as in different parts of the country for some years past, their activities being almost altogether limited to extra-institutional care of those who are either in danger of a mental breakdown or are discharged patients from state or private institutions for the insane. The possibilities for good work inherent in these organizations or societies for the social care of the insane will be dealt with at length in a subsequent chapter.

X. DIAGNOSIS OF ADMISSIONS TO STATE HOSPITALS

Mention has already been made of the difficulties encountered in attempting to supply an adequate definition of the term "insanity," and of the disagreement among students of psychiatry regarding a proper scheme or system of classification of the forms of mental alienation. These perplexities extend to the field of diagnosis of mental cases as well; in the tables that follow there will be found indications of a marked variance in the number of cases diagnosed and classified under particular divisions, in the ratio of cases reported as recovered and improved, *etc.*, even in the statistics for two of the largest of the metropolitan hospitals.

As long ago as 1874 Maudsley wrote:

> It would certainly be vastly convenient and would save a world of trouble, if it were possible to draw a hard and fast line, and to declare that all persons who were on one side of it must be sane and all persons who were on the other side of it must be insane. But a very little consideration will show how vain it is to attempt to make such a division. That nature makes no leaps, but passes from one complexion to its opposite by a gradation so gentle that one shades imperceptibly into another, and no one can fix positively the point of transition, is a sufficiently trite observation. Nowhere is this more true than in respect to sanity and insanity; it is unavoidable therefore that doubts, disputes, and perplexities should arise in dealing with particular cases.[1]

Since this statement was originally written psychiatry has advanced in leaps and bounds, and more scientific methods of diagnosis have been evolved; however, the possibility of erring on the part of the individual making and recording observations is well known, particularly in the proper interpretation of given facts. The engagement of experts

[1] Maudsley, Henry, *Responsibility in Mental Disease*, 1874, pp. 38-39.

in the diagnosis of mental diseases by both sides in murder cases, and the usual conflicting testimony is a state of affairs which has existed for a long time and doubtless will continue, so long as the standards according to which diagnoses of mental disorders are made, are not sufficiently developed to remove much of the possibility of error of judgment.

XI. RESULT OF ONE YEAR OF STATE HOSPITAL CARE

It may be affirmed without fear of contradiction that no principle in psychiatry is more firmly established than the fact that early treatment of the insane based upon a correct analysis of the physical and mental conditions is the key to success.[1] The figures in the following tables represent in a way the gauge by which we can measure the ability of the state hospital staffs properly to diagnose patients, and of the hospitals to provide the proper standards of care and treatment.

TABLE 24. DISPOSITION OF PATIENTS BY STATE HOSPITALS

Disposition.	Central Islip.		Manhattan.		Totals.	
	Male.	Female.	Male.	Female.	Male.	Female.
Remaining in Hospital	101	62	127	93	228	155
Recovered Discharged.	21	25	7	10	28	35
Much Imp. and Imp. Disch	39	41	57	64	96	105
Unimproved, Discharged	4	4	10	3	14	7
Died in Hospital	18	13	49	27	67	40
Deported to other State	1	1	1	4	2	5
Not Insane	..	1	1	..	1	1
Totals	184	147	252	201	436	348

[1] Warner, Chas. G., "Reception, Examination, and Care of New Admissions," *Amer. Jo. of Ins.*, 1916-1917, p. 673.

Table 24 indicates the disposition of the patients admitted to the state hospitals, and the result of the care and treatment given to these patients during the period of one year. These figures show that at the end of the first year of care and treatment in the two state hospitals mentioned above, of the total admissions, there were 163 or 49.2 per cent of the patients still under care in Central Islip State Hospital, and 220 or 48.5 per cent in the Manhattan State Hospital. A word should be said at this point regarding the figures for Kings Park State Hospital; the admissions to this institution from Bellevue Hospital are altogether cases which have suffered a relapse and which it is found advisable to return to the institution where they have previously been confined. Also, the number of such patients for the entire year is so small that no dependable statistics can be drawn up.

The table that follows points out the rate of recovery and improvement of patients committed to the Central Islip and Manhattan State Hospitals:

TABLE 25. RATE OF RECOVERY AND IMPROVEMENT OF PATIENTS

State Hospitals.	Recovered.						Much Improved and Improved.					
	No.			Per cent of Total Admitted.			No.			Per cent of Total Admitted.		
	Male.	Female.	Total.	Male.	Female.	Total.	Male.	Female.	Total.	Male.	Female.	Total.
Central Islip	21	25	46	11.4	17.0	13.9	39	41	80	15.7	27.9	24.1
Manhattan	7	10	17	2.7	4.9	3.8	57	64	121	22.6	31.8	27.2

The general average rate of recovery based on all admissions was 19.4 per cent for the year 1918, the rate for the males being 18.2 per cent and for the females 20.7 per cent.[1] From the figures presented above, it is quite evident that the recovery rate for the Jewish patients was unduly small, for while the per cent of the total admissions recovered for Central Islip was 20.3, for Jewish patients it was only 13.9 per cent; and whereas the rate of recoveries for Manhattan State Hospital for the year 1918 was 15.1 per cent, for the Jewish cases it was only 3.8 per cent, an abnormally low figure. The question naturally arises as to why there should be such a marked discrepancy between the rate of recovery for all patients and the rate for a particular group. Some reasons have already been given, though in connection with the discussion of another phase of the subject.

To recapitulate, it might be well to mention the fact that so many of the Jewish patients who find their way into the state hospitals do not speak English sufficiently well to permit the physicians who care for and treat them in the hospitals to recognize when the patients have recovered. The result is that a number of Jewish patients are discharged as improved or much improved, when by the method of classification adopted in the institutions many of them might properly be signed out as recovered. The figures of the improved and much improved cases seem to bear out this statement. The general rate for patients discharged, improved and much improved, based on all admissions, was 20.0 in 1918 and 18.6 per cent in 1917, while the rate for Jewish patients admitted to Central Islip and Manhattan State Hospitals was 24.1 for the former and 27.2 per cent for the latter, for the year 1918. During this

[1] S. H. C., 30th A. R., p. 307.

year the general rate for Central Islip was 21.9 per cent, and for Manhattan 21.7 per cent. After making due allowance for the larger number of Jewish patients discharged as improved and much improved, there still remains a wide margin between the total rate of recoveries and the small rate for Jewish cases. The fact that Jewish patients do not get along so well as do other patients in state hospitals has already been mentioned and Table 25 brings out this condition more clearly.

XII. FOLLOW-UP WORK IN NEW YORK CITY

(a) *Need for This Form of Service.* At this point it might be advisable to consider in brief a problem which has much bearing upon the question of the final disposition of the patients. Little need be said regarding those patients who are suffering from a more or less chronic ailment, necessitating their detention in the institutions. Table 24 brings out that of a total of 784 commitments, 383 or 48.8 per cent of the patients were still in the hospitals at the end of one year, with the probability that many would remain inmates of state institutions for many more years, and in some cases even until they died. The patients whom it is necessary to consider in greater detail however, particularly from the point of view of this study, are included in the recovered, much improved and improved groups. Experience of several years in the work of a mental hygiene agency has conclusively proved to the writer the importance of closely following-up and supervising patients thus discharged. They required advice and guidance in obtaining employment, in being directed into new and more suitable occupations, and in making those numerous readjustments which are essential to the mental well-being of former inmates of state hospitals, if relapses are to be prevented and the possibility of the development of a chronic mental disorder is to be eliminated. Moreover, the patients should be made to feel that trained psychiatrists and social workers are always available to aid them in their difficulties, whether mental, medical or social.

(b) *Extent of Follow-up Work in New York.* The state, largely through the continued activities of the State Charities Aid Association and its committee on mental hygiene, has come to realize the genuine opportunities for service inherent in a system of after-care work and has accordingly made some provisions along these lines. But to what extent has this been done, and, how much has been accomplished? In view of the possibilities for financial saving alone, not considering at this moment the more humane aspects of the problem, the state has been very lax in failing to provide a sufficiently large corps of workers to follow up discharged and paroled patients and so help to prevent relapses. A very important additional service might be rendered by these workers in spreading educational propaganda where it was most needed, namely, in the families of those who have already suffered a mental breakdown.

According to the Thirtieth Annual Report of the State Hospital Commission, the number of patients on parole on June 30, 1918, was 1,880;[1] this does not of course include those whose parole period of six months had expired. For the large number of patients technically considered as being out on parole there were only thirteen social workers in the service of the state, for whose salaries and maintenance—the only two items in the after-care budget—less than $20,000 was spent, out of a total annual budget of over $8,000,000. The actual accomplishment of this small body of workers was as follows: 3,418 visits to paroled patients,

[1] S. H. C., 30th A. R., p. 238.

(an average of less than two visits to each patient on parole); 727 visits to other patients outside the hospital; 1,841 other visits on behalf of patients, and 245 visits in behalf of preventive cases. Situations were obtained for 132 patients from the hospital and for eleven preventive cases.[1] More recently arrangements have been made by the State Hospital Commission to provide one after-care worker for every 100 patients on parole. Apropos of this welcome addition to the staff, it is of interest to note that the social service department of the Boston Psychopathic Hospital does not assign more than 20 or 25 patients to each worker.

There is no intention to disparage the good work of the follow-up staff of the state hospitals; it is desired, rather, to point out its inadequacy. The whole situation regarding this particular phase of the problem was well summarized by one of these workers when she stated that she hardly had the time to keep track of the names of those discharged and paroled, much less to serve them. This is probably a somewhat extreme statement, though it reflects the state of mind of the follow-up agents who are serving the state in the different hospitals as best they can considering the handicaps under which they labor.

(c) *Need for Follow-Up of Jewish Patients.* Table 25 indicates that 63 Jewish patients were discharged as recovered from the Central Islip and Manhattan State Hospitals, that 201 were paroled as much improved and improved, and that 21 were taken home by relatives in an unimproved condition. This makes a total of 285 patients who left these institutions during the year to return to their homes and previous environment, with but very little, if any, supervision and follow-up work. If action on the part of the state in appropriating sufficient funds for the

[1] S. H. C., 30th A. R., p. 237.

establishment of large and well organized social service staffs in the several state hospitals is as slow in materializing as it has been heretofore, the question arises as to whether it would not be advisable that some properly officered and equipped Jewish agency assist the state in following up and serving these patients, all of whom are residents of the City of New York. A further alternative presents itself, namely, that some mental hygiene agency already functioning among Jewish patients, or one to be organized on a much larger scale, be requested by the state hospital authorities to take over the work of rendering social service to the Jewish discharges. Some arrangement might be perfected whereby Jewish social workers and psychiatrists who understand the unique Jewish psychology could assist the state social workers and augment the service and assistance now being rendered.

The entire problem of after-care work among Jewish patients is one that should and must in the near future be brought to the serious attention both of the state authorities charged with the proper care of the insane, and of representatives of Jewish organizations and agencies prepared to render this particular kind of service. In order that the abnormally high readmission rate prevalent among Jewish patients of state hospitals be materially reduced through timely and adequate mental hygiene service, some such action is imperative.

XIII. DEATHS IN STATE HOSPITALS

(a) *Death Rates of Jewish Patients.* Those who are engaged in some form of service in the psychopathic wards of general hospitals to which insane or alleged insane persons are brought prior to their commitment, are frequently asked by the friends and relatives of these patients what the possibilities are for the recovery of committed cases. The facts regarding the rate of discharges and recoveries have already been noted. Table 24 shows the number of patients who were otherwise disposed of, particularly those who died in the institutions. Of the total of 784 admissions there were 107 deaths, a death rate equivalent to 13.6 per cent of the admissions; of 436 males admitted during the year, 67 or 15.3 per cent died, and of 348 females admitted in the same period, 40 or 11.5 per cent died. It is at the present time difficult to draw any valid comparisons between the death rate for Jewish admissions and for the total admissions to the several state hospitals, this being altogether due to the fact that the statistics prepared for all the patients are based not upon the admissions for the given year, but upon the total number of patients under treatment during the year. Thus, in 1918, the death rate per 1,000 patients under treatment excluding transfers, which are comparatively few in number, was 85.5; the male death rate was 98.9, and the female rate 73.5. The one point of comparison is the higher death rate indicated for males in both groups of figures.

(b) *Reasons for Increasing Death Rates.* Somewhat debatable ground is entered when considering what significance is to be attached to the fact that the death rate per 1,000 patients under treatment for all the hospitals has been slowly but definitely increasing from year to year, a condition found to exist ever since accurate statistics bearing on this phase of hospital care for the insane have been kept. In the year 1897 the total rate, that is, including males and females, was 66.0 per 1,000 patients under treatment; in 1917 it had increased to 88.8, with a somewhat lower rate for 1918, namely 85.5. The irrefutable fact is that the death rate has been increasing though the reasons therefor are not so obvious. The increasing tendency to send cases of acute mental illness to state hospitals has probably contributed to this condition. The ability in recent years more readily and accurately to diagnose cases of general paralysis, as well as other psychoses with high death rates, has resulted in the commitment of such cases to state hospitals. For instance, the highest death rates per 1,000 patients under treatment were found among patients suffering with general paralysis, the rate in 1918 having been 352.8; for cerebral arteriosclerosis the death rate was 340.2 during the same year. Furthermore, up to the last decade of the nineteenth century many cases of senile psychosis were housed in county institutions, whereas at present all such cases as reach public institutions are committed to state hospitals. When it is realized that for cases of senile psychosis the death rate per 1,000 patients under treatment in a given year, as in 1918, was 297.2, it is at once seen why the general death rate has increased so much in more recent years. The factors just mentioned have undoubtedly been largely responsible for the increased death rate, though the sum total of their effect upon the statistical averages must to some extent, at least, be neutralized by the better and higher standard of care accorded to state hospital patients during the past twenty or more years, with the resultant increase in the length of life of large numbers of patients.

The following table shows that those who died suffering from general paralysis were 43 in number, equivalent to 40.1 per cent of the total number of deaths; [1] the deaths from senile psychosis numbered 20, or 18.6 per cent of the total deaths.

[1] Dublin, Louis I., *Mortality Statistics of Insured Wage-Earners and their Families*, 1919, pp. 271-272, presents a discussion of death rates among a large number of insured persons where the cause of death was general paralysis.

TABLE 26. DIAGNOSIS OF PATIENTS WHO DIED IN STATE HOSPITALS

Diagnosis.	Central Islip.		Manhattan.		Total.	
	Male.	Female.	Male.	Female.	Male.	Female.
General Paralysis	7	2	30	4	37	6
Senile Psychosis	4	2	4	10	8	12
Arteriosclerosis	1	2	2	2	3	4
Manic Depressive	2	6	6	4	8	10
Dementia Praecox	2	..	3	5	5	5
Epileptic Psychosis	2	..	3	..	5	..
Constitutionally Psy. Inf.	..	1	..	..	..	1
Involutional Melancholia	..	..	..	1	..	1
Infection Exhaustion Psy.	..	..	..	1	..	1
Intoxication Psychosis	..	..	1	..	1	..
Totals	18	13	49	27	67	40

The total number of cases admitted during the year and diagnosed as afflicted with general paralysis was 99, out of which as already noted, 43 died within the year. This gives a death rate of approximately 400 out of 1,000 such patients admitted within the year, a figure somewhat higher than the death rate for all the patients similarly diagnosed. The death rate for the senile cases was about the same as the rate for all the cases classified under this diagnosis.

XIV. LENGTH OF STAY IN THE HOSPITALS

Reference has already been made in explanation of Table 25 to the difference between Central Islip and Manhattan State Hospitals in the ratio of patients signed out as "recovered"; in analyzing the above figures the statements referred to should be taken into consideration. This table furthermore emphasizes the facts noted in Chapter II regarding the recovery rate of the different psychoses, parti-

TABLE 27. DURATION OF HOSPITAL LIFE OF RECOVERED CASES

	M. D. I.	Cons. Inf.	Para. Cond.	D. P. Kat.	All Others.	Totals.	
	No.	No.	No.	No.	No.	No.	Per cent.
Less than 1 month	2	..	..	..	..	2	3.1
1 to 3 months........	15	4	1	1	3	24	38.1
4 to 7 months........	21	4	..	1	..	26	41.3
8 to 11 months........	11	..	..	..	..	11	17.5
Totals	49	8	1	2	3	63	100.0

cularly the comparatively higher rate among cases of manic depressive insanity. It is seen that nearly all patients who recovered had suffered with manic depressive insanity; the eight cases included as cases of constitutional inferiority suffered depressions similar in nature to those usually included under the category of manic depressive insanity, depressed type, the depression coming in addition to the constitutional ailment. Recoveries of cases of dementia praecox, katatonic type, are very rare, and some authorities are inclined to the opinion that often such cases as are recorded as having recovered have been inaccurately diagnosed in the hospitals from which they have been discharged in a recovered or even improved condition. Their contention is that the patients thus diagnosed were suffering from some condition of stupor and were not true cases of katatonic dementia praecox. Be that as it may, the number of recorded recoveries is so small as to be almost negligible.[1]

Table 28 serves the double purpose of indicating the diagnoses of the improved and much improved cases, and of showing the duration of hospital life of the patients classi-

[1] de Fursac and Rosanoff, *Manual of Psychiatry*, p. 262.

TABLE 28. DURATION OF HOSPITAL LIFE OF IMPROVED AND MUCH IMPROVED CASES

	M. D. I.	D. P.	G. P.	Sen. Psy.	Art. Scler.	Epil. Psy.	Const. Inf.	All Others.	Totals.	
	No.	No.	No.	No.	No.	No.	No.	No.	No.	Per cent.
Less than 1 month.....	14	1	..	1	1	2	..	3	22	10.9
1 to 3 months.........	36	14	4	2	2	4	3	6	71	35.5
4 to 7 months.........	37	27	1	2	2	1	3	9	82	40.8
8 to 11 months.........	7	13	1	1	1	..	..	3	26	12.8
Totals...........	94	55	6	6	6	7	6	21	201	100.0

fied in these two groups. There were 94 cases of manic depressive insanity paroled, to which should be added the 49 cases of the same diagnosis included in Table 27 as recovered, making a total of 143 patients diagnosed as manic depressives discharged as recovered or improved. From Table 5 it is seen that 294 such cases were originally committed to state hospitals, out of which 143 or 48.6 per cent were discharged as recovered or in an improved condition. Two hundred and seventy-nine cases of dementia praecox were committed to state hospitals; of this number two presumably recovered and 55 were discharged as improved, these 57 cases being equivalent to 20.4 per cent of the total commitments. Of the cases of general paralysis, senile psychosis and cerebral arteriosclerosis, the three groups in which the highest proportion of deaths occur, there were, as might properly be expected, no recoveries at all, while each group indicated improved conditions in six cases. There were seven patients discharged as improved who had been diagnosed as suffering from epileptic psychosis, and six diagnosed as cases of constitutional psychopathic inferiority were similarly discharged.

Regarding the duration of hospital life of improved and much improved discharges, it is to be noted from Table 28 that 10.9 per cent of the discharges took place within the first month of hospital residence; 35.5 per cent were sent home in from one to three months, 40.8 per cent were detained from four to seven months, and 12.8 per cent from eight to eleven months. The indications therefore are that it should take from one to seven months of institutional life before approximately 80 per cent of the patients discharged as in an improved condition will be permitted to leave the hospitals on parole. With better hospital conditions obtaining in the state institutions, with less overcrowding, and a higher ratio of physicians and nurses to the number of patients under treatment, the duration of hospital residence for presumably recoverable cases would undoubtedly be shortened, with a resultant decrease in the general cost of operation and maintenance of the hospitals. Even if the increased cost of managing the state hospitals after making these changes went far to offset the decrease in cost of maintenance as a result of earlier discharges, yet the added expenditure would be sufficiently justified by the fact that patients could be returned to normal environments and to their families and friends weeks if not months sooner than at present.

It is noticed from Table 29 that the majority of the deaths occured within four months of admission to the state hospitals and that 86.9 per cent died in less than eight months. Those showing the shortest length of life within the institutions were the cases of general paralysis, about 75 per cent of which died in less than four months of institutional residence. Coupled with the fact that 43.4 per cent of the total number of admissions of paretics died within the year, it is evident that the menace of general paralysis to the duration of life is exceedingly threatening. The high rate

TABLE 29. DURATION OF HOSPITAL LIFE OF PATIENTS DYING IN STATE HOSPITALS

	G. P.	Sen. Psy.	M. D. I.	D. P.	Art. Scl.	Epil. Psy.	All Others.	Totals.	
	No.	No.	No.	No.	No.	No.	No.	No.	Per cent.
Less than 1 month	13	3	8	2	2	1	..	29	27.1
1 to 3 months..............	19	7	4	2	4	..	3	39	36.4
4 to 7 months..............	7	7	3	3	1	3	1	25	23.4
8 to 11 months..............	4	3	3	3	..	1	..	14	13.1
Totals.	43	20	18	10	7	5	4	107	100.0

of early deaths from manic depressive insanity is due to the fact that a certain proportion of these patients is rather prone to an early demise as a result of physical exhaustion following the occasional restraint into which these patients are put. The tendency in the New York State Hospitals, as well as in all modern and up-to-date similar institutions, has been to reduce the number of patients put into physical restraint during temporary or prolonged periods of excitement. Nevertheless, overcrowding and the inadequacy of the hospital staffs for the large number of patients under treatment occasionally necessitate the violation of a more recent conception of the methods to be employed under such circumstances—the use of hydrotherapeutic apparatus, such as the continuous bath, in the place of restraining sheets or bandages, which are but vestiges of the chain and dungeon period of the treatment of the insane.

This is but another indication of the pressing need for changes or reforms in our current methods of treating and caring for the insane, particularly the Jewish insane. Several questions have already been raised as to the advisability of continuing the present procedure of indiscriminately and regularly committing all indigent and semi-indigent Jewish patients, recoverable and otherwise, to state institutions in which they apparently do not progress along the road to recovery as well as do some other groups of patients. The evident and only conclusions that can be drawn from these facts are, either reforms must come from within, that is, from the state hospitals themselves and through the State Hospital Commission, or private organizations and agencies must enter the field and supplement or take over some of the work of the state institutions, with particular reference to so-called recoverable cases; a third alternative that suggests itself is, that there might possibly be effected a combination of the first two recommendations.

CHAPTER IV

A Social Survey of 786 Admissions to State Hospitals

I. INTRODUCTION

In the preceding chapter the attempt was made to point out the shortcomings of the state hospital system insofar as care and treatment in the hospitals themselves are concerned. As has by now become evident, this study aims to consider the patients from all angles, including the care accorded in the place of temporary confinement, particularly in Bellevue Hospital; the care and treatment in the institutions to which they are committed, *i. e.*, the state hospitals; the condition and progress of the patients discharged from the state hospitals; and the work of the after-care or parole agents of these hospitals. Before turning to a consideration of the main topics to be discussed in this chapter, it might be well to give thought to a number of social facts which this study has developed regarding the insane. In the second chapter a table of the marital condition of the patients admitted to Bellevue Hospital, psychopathic wards, was presented (Table 10). From this table it was seen that out of a total of 1,127 patients, 596 or 52.9 per cent were single, 435 or 39.6 per cent were married; and of the males, 25 patients were widowed and 8 divorced; whereas of the females, 53 patients were widowed and 10 divorced. These facts in themselves do not throw sufficient light upon the subject of social needs or upon the possibilities for service among the patients, discharged or otherwise, or among their families.

II. THE FAMILY OF THE INSANE PATIENTS

In his volume on "The Family and Social Work," Dr. Edward T. Devine points out that the methods and policies of scientifically organized charitable relief have been adopted or rejected according to their profitable effect on family standards, and that it has become an axiom that each individual who is in need of assistance must be considered in his family setting if he is to be helped effectively.[1] While this opinion emphasizes relief work, it is equally applicable to all phases of social work worthy the name. How true this is in cases of insanity is only too evident, for in but few other forms of social distress is the family more thoroughly upset and in need of proper advice and guidance. The question of the hereditary nature of insanity has a very disturbing effect on the relatives and immediate members of the family of an insane person when they learn that one of their own flesh and blood has been declared insane.

There were, as has been previously noted, 786 patients admitted to the Manhattan and Central Islip State Hospitals out of the total of 1,127 admissions to the psychopathic wards of Bellevue Hospital. In evaluating the services being rendered a community by its social agencies it is advisable, in justice to the institutions as well as to the public, that the efforts expended in ameliorating social conditions be given a fair trial. A prime factor in such procedure must necessarily be the question of the time permitted to elapse prior to the passing of judgment. It goes without saying that the problem must be very carefully followed out and studied during this time. In this connection, it has been deemed advisable to begin to survey the results of the work of the state hospitals in treating, and when possible curing patients, one year after the admission of a particular group

[1] Devine, Edward T., *The Family and Social Work*, p. 32.

to the institutions. That is, patients admitted to a state hospital on a given date have not been considered subjects for study in the sense outlined in this chapter until twelve months later.

The movement of patients, including death rates, was discussed at length in the preceding chapter and in this connection only facts essential to a proper understanding of the problem as a whole in some of its other aspects will be considered in the major portion of the pages that follow. Since this part of the study concerns itself more particularly with the social phase of the subject, and the aim is to obtain facts and arrive at conclusions relative to the social conditions of the patients and their families, using the term "social conditions" in its broadest sense, the total or 786 patients have been divided into four categories. These are (a) those still in the hospitals at the end of one year—mostly single persons—who have no dependents and no family responsibilities; (b) those still in the state hospitals at the end of one year, who, prior to their admission, had family responsibilities; (c) those who died in the hospitals, whether or not they left minor children or other dependents; and (d) those discharged from the hospitals within a year after admission.

III. SINGLE PERSONS WITHOUT DEPENDENTS, IN STATE HOSPITALS FOR ONE YEAR

Some consideration has already been given to the very large loss, economic and otherwise, sustained by society in the withdrawal from industry and gainful occupation of thousands of young persons whom it has been found necessary to commit and to detain in hospitals for the insane. Many of these patients are doomed to remain in the custody and under the supervision of the state for many years, if not for the remainder of their lives. Referring especially to the group of 786 cases already spoken of, it is interesting to note that out of this number there remained in the institutions at the end of one year 244 single persons without dependents. These were mainly young persons with a history of irregularity of employment and with only intermittent periods of gainful occupation to their credit. This may be ascribed to the fact that of the 244 single persons, 151 or 62 per cent had been diagnosed as suffering from one of the forms of dementia praecox, which, as has previously been pointed out, is at the present time considered as being largely chronic in nature. Among the remaining number of cases only 61 or 25 per cent represented patients diagnosed as cases of manic depressive insanity, usually thought of as a recoverable form of insanity.

Little need or can be said pertaining to the social conditions of these patients and their relatives. The former will remain in the hospitals until the doctors feel that they have sufficiently improved mentally to render it safe and advisable to give them the opportunity of attempting to adjust themselves in what we call a normal environment. The state and society are at the present time doing little to aid them in the stressing process of readjustment to difficult living and working conditions.

Under ordinary circumstances it would be fair to assume that in nearly every case there would be relatives and friends ready and willing, as well as prepared, to give the paroled patient every help and chance to redeem himself mentally and physically, and even socially and economically. However, many of these young people came to this country with the aim of bettering themselves, and in the attempt overworked and broke down after giving the best that was in them to the industries in which they were employed. Having arrived here alone, they usually had no one to turn to upon discharge from the hospitals. This resulted in the retardation of their full recovery and in increased difficulties in readjusting themselves to alien conditions. This particular phase of the subject will be more fully discussed in the following pages, but it may be apropos to mention at this point that there are organizations in New York that provide positions and other requisites to discharged prisoners, persons who have violated the laws of the state; and yet, for those who have fallen by the wayside as a result of illness, little if anything is attempted in the way of real help and assistance.

(a) *Value of Visits to Patients.* The patients remaining in state hospitals and having relatives are somewhat better off because of the greater attention they receive through the agency of regular visits paid them and the delicacies and other things brought to them. These are seemingly small matters, but to sensitive individuals who still retain many of their faculties, though they may be in depressed or elated or even stuporous conditions for greater or lesser periods of time, the modicum of interest displayed by visiting relatives and friends helps in the improvement of their mental condition. *Foster relatives* in the guise of social workers assigned to the state hospitals for work on the wards would go a long way towards breaking the terrible monotony of life in a state hospital, and thus help in the earlier improvement of improvable and recoverable cases. A state hospital superintendent once remarked that if a small group of normal individuals were compelled to remain within a circumscribed area, as in a ward, for any length of time, several if not all these persons would in a relatively short time begin to feel and believe that one or more of the other persons within the confined limits of the four walls had developed an antagonism and even hatred towards the others. This would resolve itself eventually into ideas of persecution and actual psychoses. If such be the case even to a limited extent among normal individuals, how much more liable to mental deterioration are persons already adjudged insane and confined in overcrowded hospitals and wards month after month and year upon year.

(b) *Attitude of Patients' Relatives toward State Hospitals.* Many visits to the homes of relatives of patients committed to state hospitals, even where such relatives have not been directly dependent upon the patients for either total or even partial support, have shown the forcefulness with which the relatives are impressed with the fact that, at least to their way of thinking, well-nigh nothing is being done to hasten the recovery of the persons detained in the hospitals by the state. The result is that the next of kin and friends are constantly insisting upon the discharge to their custody of patients who may be a menace to themselves and to others, and would certainly be a definite burden to keep at home. They feel that they can do more for the afflicted members of their families than the hospitals accomplish.

It is quite useless and of no avail to discuss with these relatives the fact, for instance, that the hospital superintendents and physicians would do more to hasten the improvement of patients if they only had the necessary funds which which to provide better accommodations, or to hire a higher grade of attendants and a larger proportion of trained nurses. It is likewise inadvisable, as a rule, to tell them, even if one always had the heart to do so, that their dear ones are suffering from a form of insanity which has to this day baffled the best minds in the field of psychiatry; and that, as far as one can truthfully say, the patients will probably never be well mentally. The only thing that can be done is to point out to relatives and friends that the doctors and nurses are doing all in their power to hasten the recovery of all patients, and to advise against the attempted withdrawal from the institutions of patients of known suicidal or homicidal or probable perverted tendencies.

IV. MARRIED, WIDOWED AND DIVORCED PERSONS, WITHOUT DEPENDENTS, REMAINING IN STATE HOSPITALS

As might naturally be expected, there were smaller numbers of married, widowed and divorced persons without dependents detained in the hospitals at the end of one year of institutional residence than there were single persons placed in this category. The statements already made regarding unmarried people apply with equal force to the three groups now being considered. In many instances, the desire to obtain the early discharge of a husband or wife, father or mother, is even more determined. The departure from the home of such a person has in numerous cases resulted in the breaking up of the household and the scattering of the remaining members. As a rule, it is only after prolonged deliberation on the part of immediate relatives that such patients are committed, this usually occurring when it is found that the entire life of the family is disturbed by the peculiar habits and behavior of those who have become mentally ill.[1] Families of very meagre income have put themselves greatly in debt so as to send such persons to high-priced private sanatoria, only to find to their dismay that at the end of a few weeks all the resources are exhausted and the patients very little improved, if improvement there has been. The result has been that these patients are finally committed to a state hospital.

V. SOCIAL STATUS OF PATIENTS WHO DIED IN STATE HOSPITALS

The ratio of the deaths to the total admissions has already

[1] Henderson, Charles R., *Dependents, Defectives and Delinquents*, 1909, p. 184.

been indicated, and the division into sexes has likewise been dwelt upon (Table 24). For purposes of convenience these figures are repeated; of the total of 784 admissions to state hospitals there were 107 deaths during the year, equivalent to a death rate of 13.6 per cent. There were 436 males admitted, of whom 67 or 15.3 per cent died, whereas of the 348 females admitted, 40 or 11.5 per cent died.

(a) *Single.* A further classification of these patients has shown that of the single persons who died, 17 were males and 9 females. From the point of view of their relation to their next of kin and the bearing such deaths had upon the immediate and future social status of the families of which they were a part, it has been found that these patients fall into five groups. The first group comprises young people who either contributed very little or nothing to the family income, often having been a serious burden and drain upon the financial resources of the family. The untimely deaths of these persons did not in any case seriously affect the status of the family; in some instances the removal of the hopelessly insane was a cause of positive relief in more ways than one. The second group is made up of workers whose loss of income will be felt by the family but not sufficiently to render appeal for financial assistance to a social agency necessary. Such families readily adjusted themselves to the lessened income. In fact, so many of these patients had been ill for varying and prolonged periods of time that while they were periodically engaged in some gainful occupation, nevertheless they represented an economic loss both from the point of view of society as a whole and of their own families in particular. In the third group are classed persons who had no immediate relatives in this country, representing almost altogether recent immigrants whose deaths could not materially affect the social status of their families in other lands. It is, of course, realized that families in European as well as other lands often pool their savings in order to help one of the more able members of the group to migrate to "the land of promise," hoping thereby to profit from the increased earnings of such as come to these shores. The question is whether in these cases loss of income and any resultant lowering of the standard of living can be properly gauged, as we presumably can only surmise the effects of the death of adult wage-earners. Furthermore, from the point of view of the problem here in this state and country, these cases are negligible factors, at least insofar as our standards are affected and the welfare of future citizens involved. Stress has already been laid upon the social drain incurred through the loss of efficiency and health as well as of life itself by those who become infected with syphilis and such of their number who eventually develop general paralysis. These constitute the fourth group. Of the single persons dying of this disease, none bore any definite family responsibilities. They were largely individuals who had either become alienated or otherwise separated from their families years before their deaths took place and whose loss was not seriously felt by relatives, except perhaps for the sympathetic reaction exerted upon kith and kin. The last group represents deaths of single persons of advanced years from senile psychosis. Such deaths would naturally be expected to affect the social status of few, if any, persons.

(b) *Married.* It is interesting to note that married persons dying in the state hospitals contributed 62 out of 107 deaths; of these 41 were males and 21 females. The possible social needs to be uncovered by a careful study of families of wage-earners in which either the father or mother have died would necessitate a discussion in great detail of almost every social agency operating in a community, coupled with an appraisal of the efficiency with which service has been rendered in the comparatively large number of cases being considered. The purpose of this work being rather to point out the social implications of the problem of insanity as a whole, and not to limit its scope to a study of particular cases only, it is obvious that the aim in view could not be realized within the confines of a single volume unless some necessary limitations were set. And so, instead of considering at length all details of the problems found to be involved in the cases being studied under this heading, it is taken for granted that certain factors are only touched upon and it is left to the reader to follow out in greater detail by reference to standard works on the subject, such particular interests as may be awakened by a perusal of these pages.

(c) *Status of Family Following Death of Husband.* Analysis of the social histories of the married persons who died in the state hospitals shows that they fall into several classes. Of the males dying there were those who left behind them:

(a) a wife and wage-earning adult children.
(b) a wife of advanced years taken in by relatives or aided by a relief organization.
(c) a wife and minor children, all aided by relatives.
(d) a wife and minor children aided by a relief organization as husband and father was not a citizen, thereby disqualifying children from receiving a pension.
(e) a wife, childless, living apart from husband the latter part of his lifetime, because of his physical and mental condition.
(f) a wife, with minor children, self-supporting, because of a small business operated by the mother.
(g) a wife, childless, working and self-supporting for a number of years prior to death of husband.

(h) a wife with minor children, working several years prior to death of husband, and supporting the entire family.

(i) a wife and minor children, latter cared for by relatives while mother went out working, even during the lifetime of husband.

(j) a wife and children, family with independent means and in comfortable circumstances.

(k) a wife and minor children, recipients of a pension, father having been a citizen.

(l) a wife in a state hospital and children all adults.

(m) a wife and children in Europe.

(d) *Status of Family Following Death of Wife.* A consideration of the cases in which the mother of the family died would quite naturally be expected to indicate fewer instances in which financial aid or assistance was needed, but other forms of social service had to be called upon to meet the emergency created through the death of the mother of minor children. The analysis of the deaths among married females shows that they might be classified as follows from the point of view of social need discovered in the families:

(a) minor children cared for by relatives other than the father.

(b) husband being cared for by adult children, patient having died at an advanced age leaving no dependents.

(c) husband boarding out the minor children.

(d) husband committing children to an orphan asylum.

(e) husband alone remaining; childless marriage.

(f) husband unable properly to care for children during illness of wife, and children placed with relatives.

(g) husband in army when wife died; children placed with relatives by Home Service Section, American Red Cross.

It is of course realized that the instances above enumerated in regard to both the male and the female married patients dying in the institutions do not exhaust the list of possible circumstances in which the families might have been left, but they do represent the actual conditions in which a number of families were found. The groups under study are particularly interesting from the social point of view because they represent almost entirely persons of wage-earning families and very few, if any, of large or comparatively large business or other holdings.

VI. SOCIAL PROBLEMS FOLLOWING DEATH OF MARRIED PATIENTS

Attention has already been paid to the desirability as well as to the necessity of considering the patients from the point of view of their place in a given family, if constructive work is to be done for the patients as well as for those related to them by ties of blood. This particular part of the discussion deals with patients who have passed beyond all possible aid and relief, and have left behind them heritages which are not always social assets. In his volume on the *Psychic Treatment of Nervous Disorders*,[1] Dr. Dubois states that in the treatment of such ailments, it is essential not to confine one's therapeutic effort to the patients alone, but to extend it to those who live with them. The family must be considered as the ultimate unit of our social organization,[2] and any plans for the social treatment of one member of the group must take into consideration the effect of such treatment upon the other members of the family, for the good results of individual treatment often crumble away before the onslaughts of difficult and complex group or

[1] Dubois, Paul, *Psychic Treatment of Nervous Disorders*, 1909, p. 44.

[2] Devine, *Principles of Relief*, 1904, p. 77.

family problems. Just as in medicine, so in the field of social science, our patients and their families must be thought of as integral parts of a given whole.

(a) *Death of Aged Married Men.* Turning to the deaths of husbands and fathers, and the effect of their demise upon the family life and structure, it is quite apparent that family conditions are but slightly affected when a man of advanced years dies, leaving a widow and several adult children. In the instances in which this happened, the children assumed the burden of supporting the entire household, their only task being the support of an aged mother with few and simple wants. The presumption is that the family structure will continue as before the death of the patient. until, through the natural withdrawal of the children to establish new families of their own, it is found advisable to take the widowed mother into the household of one of the children. The death of a man of advanced years, leaving a widow of about the same age but no children, involves problems of a more complex nature than the mere adjustment of family affairs following in the wake of the previous instance. There are three alternatives to choose from; either relatives must support or take into their homes such widows, or they can be aided financially by a relief organization and allowed to board with friends, or provision must be found for them in some home for the aged. None of the wives of the patients considered under this heading found their way into institutions, as they were either taken in by relatives or subsidized by a relief organization.

(b) *Care of Dependent Widows and Orphans.* Most of the serious social problems following upon the deaths of married men would naturally fall in the families in which there were one or more minor children left to the care of a penniless mother. Analysis has shown that in these cases relatives in comfortable circumstances sometimes came to the rescue of the family in distress, making all the necessary provision for their sustenance and comfort. It is the proverbial way of caring for such dependents, and self-sacrificing relatives of this calibre are fully deserving of the thanks of the community, even though such service should be looked upon as a duty and an obligation rather than as a favor. The difficulty is, however, that few of the patients admitted to the psychopathic wards of Bellevue Hospital and subsequently to the state hospitals have immediate relatives in a position to assume such serious financial obligations. The result has been that in instances where the deceased was not a citizen and the widow was left with no estate and several minor children, she has had to wend her way to a relief organization for the support of her children and herself, until such time as they became of wage-earning age.

The effect of sexual disease in the husband upon the sterility of his wife is a well-recognized phenomenon, and it is not surprising therefore that there were a number of childless widows of men dying in the state hospitals, largely with a diagnosis of general paralysis. Wives learning the true mental and physical conditions of their husbands have in many instances left them in order to earn their own livelihoods; or, where the affection of the wife for the husband was not sufficiently destroyed to lead her to desert the sick and suffering man, she has gone out to work as soon as his inability further to support her and himself became apparent.

Fortunately for some of the widows and their half-orphaned children, the husbands and fathers had operated and owned some small retail business and it was out of the income from this source that several of the families managed to support themselves, sometimes with the occasional financial assistance of kind friends and relatives. Mental disease often incapacitates persons for a long period of time, with the result that they become unable properly to discharge their family responsibilities. In a number of cases where there was a combination of a wife and minor children and a husband and father too ill mentally to work regularly, the wife has gone into industry to earn sufficient to keep the family together. She has either left the children at home under the care of a father who suffered from periodic attacks of mental instability and alienation, or has placed them in day nurseries or with friends and relatives until her return from the shop and factory. The inadvisability of permitting such a father to be the guardian of the young children throughout the day is quite obvious, but no agency is as yet prepared to take care of the large number of cases in which this and similar incidents are of almost daily occurrence. This is but another indication of the need of concerted action throughout the community if the problem of the insane and their families is to be solved along empirical and rational lines. At present such family problems are met in the best way known to the immediate relatives and friends, sometimes with the aid of a social agency unacquainted with the special and peculiar problems involved in the adjustment for any long or short period of time, of the dependents of a mentally unbalanced husband and father.

Families in which the father has died in a state hospital leaving a wife and minor children, and also means sufficient to maintain the family in comfort, present few problems needing solution. It has been found however, that often the relatives are in need of advice regarding the probable effect, if any, of insanity in the father upon the children. In instances in which the father died of general paralysis the utility of Wasserman tests performed upon all immediate members of the family is readily apparent, and invariably information of this nature given to relatives has been welcomed and quite frequently followed out.

Similar to the foregoing instance are the cases in which the father was a citizen and where consequently the mother was granted a pension on behalf of her minor and dependent children. There is a difference, however, in that in the latter cases the families may be in need of financial assistance to tide them over until their case is finally passed upon by the Board of Child Welfare and is placed on the pension role. Some instances occurred in which the wife herself was a patient in a state hospital for the insane, though no minor children were left to need the attention of a social agency. Had there been such children the obvious plan would have been, as in similar situations in which both parents are either dead or mentally incompetent, to place them with relatives, or for a child-caring agency to provide for them in an orphan asylum or to board them out.

The waves of immigration in the years preceding the war brought large numbers of single as well as married men to this country. Many of the latter, however, arrived here alone in order to establish a home for their families whom they had left in some European land, their plan being to send for their wives and children as soon as they had saved sufficient to pay for the passage of their families and for the new household they intended to establish. Unfortunately for some, the plans so well thought out went wrong, due altogether to the fact that the father became mentally unbalanced before he could send for the family. Such cases are indeed sad, though there is nothing that can be done either for the family or for the patient, as the latter has to be considered as a single man without any family responsibilities, at least during the period of his illness. The question of deportation is of course involved in some instances, though it was found that most of these patients had been in this country beyond the five-year limit and had not become public charges prior to that time.

(c) *Family Problems following Death of Mothers.* In the cases in which the mother of the family died, it is quite conceivable that a widower, upon his wife's death, should find himself seriously embarrassed in making provision for the care of his children, even though his income had been sufficient to care for the entire family. As is well recognized, in the normal family the contribution made by the mother to the common welfare is often fully equal to that of the father even though it is not so readily measured in dollars and cents. The loss of the mother does not necessarily cause the family of the wage-earner to become dependent upon outside financial aid, though the assistance of social agencies interested in the care and welfare of children is often necessary. Due often to particular family conditions, the father is not able properly to care and provide for his orphaned children, and he is thus compelled to turn to others for help. The natural thing is that he should first of all appeal either to his own or to his deceased wife's relatives, so that his children may be quickly provided with a proper home and suitable accommodations essential for their future well-being. In several of the families studied it was the relatives who came to the help of the children, either because of the strength of family ties or as a result of the father's inability for one reason or another properly to provide for his children.

Sometimes the opposite kind of situation developed; instead of care being needed for the children, the aged father had to be provided for by his adult children. This never involved any serious social problem, for the children usually took the father into their own home or made other provisions for his maintenance and welfare.

Emphasis has been placed upon the advisability of maintaining the family as a unit whenever possible. The placing-out of children either in institutions or in boarding homes is only a make-shift to meet a condition of affairs for which there seemingly is no better way. In many instances far better results are obtained if one of the children, especially if a daughter, is old enough to take up the household cares, or if some near relative of the family is in a position to step into the vacant place. During the first few months following the deaths of a number of the mothers, the husbands had to resort to the expedient of boarding out the minor children because of inability to make any adjustments which would have resulted in the maintenance of the family under one roof. Other fathers found it necessary to have their minor children committed to orphan asylums, as they did not earn sufficient to support their several children either in their own homes or in foster or boarding homes. The financial arrangement always insisted upon by the Department of Public Welfare of the City of New York is that the father must regularly pay a certain amount per week to the Department for the maintenance and support of his children, the amount depending upon the number of children committed and the average earnings of the father. A number of the husbands eventually re-married and took their children of the first marriage with them into the new household, thus making as suitable provision for their care as the circumstances would allow.

Childless marriages have always been regarded by one school of thought as unnatural and uncalled-for, particularly when both the husband and wife are in good mental and physical condition and are in a position properly or at least adequately to provide for such offspring as they may have. In those cases in which the wife died without leaving any children, the husband had no family problems needing solution, and he returned to the status of a single man.

From the point of view of society as a whole, it was probably fortunate that a few of the married women who died in hospitals for the insane left no progeny, for, even from the little we know at present regarding the inheritance of mental disease, it is quite probable that at least some of the children, had they been born, would have become afflicted with some form of mental or nervous ailment.

The exact classification of social phenomena is frequently fraught with much difficulty, particularly when the groups for various reasons are limited in number. In several cases in which the wife and mother died in the state hospital, the husband had not been able to and did not provide and care for his children even prior to the time of the death of his wife. There were a number of causes for this, among them being the illness of the father, lack of sufficient earnings, desertion, *etc.* The action taken by the relatives of the couples in several such families was to have the children placed with grandparents or other immediate relatives during the illness of the mother, and remain in such homes after the mother's death. There were one or two cases in which the mother died in a state hospital during the time that the husband and father was serving in the army. The Home Service Section of the American Red Cross readily came to the assistance of the dependent children by placing them in boarding homes until the fathers returned home.

(d) *Widowed.* The total number of widowed persons dying in state hospitals was rather small, numbering 7 males and 10 females. The social problems presented by this group were almost insignificant, due altogether to the fact that of the males, the ages at death were between 55 and 80 years, while of the 10 females, 9 ranged in age between 68 and 89 years; the tenth patient was a widow of 33 years, whose two minor children had been placed with relatives some time prior to her death as she had been ill for a long time previous to her admission to the state hospital. None of the aged widowers or widows left any dependents, as such children as they had were all self-supporting adults.

(e) *Divorced.* There were only two cases of divorced persons dying in the state hospitals, and both of these were men who had been sick for many years prior to their admission to the institution in which they passed away. Under the divorce laws of the State of New York a divorce can be granted only for infidelity. On grounds of insanity the marriage, under certain conditions, may be annulled. From the facts in hand regarding these two cases it appears that in one a divorce was obtained by the wife in another country; in the other, though the patient claimed at the time of his admission to the psychopathic ward of Bellevue Hospital that he had been divorced by his wife, it was later determined that she had only obtained a separation from him.

(f) *Modification of Marriage and Divorce Laws.* The injustice of the stringent divorce laws of New York State to the innocent party to a marriage in which one of the participants at an early date or even eventually becomes hopelessly insane, is apparent to all students of social problems. The time is overdue when New York should follow in the footsteps of other states and liberalize the obsolete and unfair laws relating to divorce. In no group of social facts that can be presented is this more strongly evidenced than in a consideration of the misery and unhappiness and blasted lives of young manhood and young womanhood following insanity in a young married person. Marriage licenses in New York contain the following statement which both parties are required to sign: " I have not to my knowledge been infected with any venereal disease or if I have been so infected within five years, I have had a laboratory test within that period which shows that I am now free from infection from any such disease." A further statement might well be added to marriage licenses—one which would inform the healthy partner to a marriage contract of former attacks of insanity in the other.

VII. PAROLE SYSTEM OF STATE HOSPITALS

Before discussing the discharged cases and the facts brought out as a result of following them up some time subsequent to their discharge from the state hospitals, it might be well to present the outstanding features of the parole and out-patient departments of the state hospitals. It is to these departments that discharged patients are referred and to which they are expected to report during the parole period, usually of six months, though occasionally of longer duration.

(a) *Development of Out-Patient Departments.* In 1913 the legislature, at the suggestion of the State Charities Aid Association, passed a law authorizing each of the state hospitals to establish an out-patient department, assign a physician to it and employ a field agent or social worker. At that time this law was referred to by competent authority as the most important law in behalf of the insane passed in a generation.[1] It was some years, however, before all the thirteen state hospitals had organized this branch or department of their work and engaged the services of a social worker. Had sufficient funds been available and the new activity been initiated with more vigor, it is apparent that a considerable number of persons who eventually were committed to the state hospitals because of the lack of competent advice or early treatment would have been saved the rather unpleasant experience of residence as patients in a state hospital for the insane.

[1] S. H. C., 28th A. R., p. 352.

The out-patient departments and the parole activities of the state hospitals are naturally inter-related, for it is to the clinics established under the law of 1913 that the parole patients report; and similarly, the social worker assigned to the out-patient department also looks after the parole cases. The effects of the mental clinics upon the hospitals are several; they provide a means whereby the hospital can supply medical supervision to its patients even when they live at a distance from the institution itself; they provide an inconspicuous place to which sensitive patients are willing to come when they would hesitate to return to the hospital; and also, by giving parole patients an opportunity regularly and frequently to see a physician who understands them, the hospital is enabled to keep a number of patients on parole who would otherwise have to return. The clinics are also of value to the hospital physician, as he is given the opportunity to do preventive work and meet types of cases in the milder forms which rarely reach the state hospital.[1] There would be little hesitancy in denominating such a system of out-patient and parole departments of state hospitals a great force and factor in preventive work and of the highest form of medical and social usefulness, provided only that its standard of service and effectiveness was high. Whether or not such is the case at present may be readily judged from the facts presented in the following paragraphs.

(b) *Extent and Effectiveness of Parole System.* The procedure followed by the writer in attempting to arrive at a fair and at the same time convincing conclusion as to the value and usefulness of the out-patient and parole activities, was to consult the parole records of the patients discharged from both the Manhattan and Central Islip State

[1] *The Parole System of New York State Hospitals*, published by New York State Charities Aid Assn., Nov., 1917.

Hospitals, limiting the study however, to those cases which have been considered in the preceding chapters. There was some difficulty in attempting to carry out this plan, due altogether to the fact that the field agent or social worker attached to one of the hospitals frankly admitted that her routine work was so heavy and the number of parole patients so large, that she had been unable to keep any records of value during the time to which this study is limited. A year later, with some clerical assistance, she was in a better position to keep some kind of record for each patient out on parole, usually not more than a note by the examining physician that the patient reported at the clinic and was discharged from parole on a given date. The records of the clinics of the other hospital were somewhat more complete, due to the fact that the social worker had a sufficient knowledge of stenography and typewriting to enable her to take the dictation of the clinic physician and transcribe the notes into the records of the patients reporting at the clinics. Following are excerpts taken from the parole records of several patients:

In the case of patient No. 13,671 the report read, "He (the patient) does not agree that the abnormal sexual sensations are any less since he left the hospital; conversation tends to be quite disconnected and poorly constructed. His parole is due to expire in a few days and he is discharged from the clinic."

In No. 14,011, a case of dementia praecox, katatonic type, the clinical report stated that the patient was childish and not fully recovered; also that "his condition is of course far from satisfactory, but his parole having expired three days ago, nothing can be done except to discharge him from the clinic." This patient was engaged to be married at the time of his last visit to the clinic, and the notes quoted were written at that time.

No. 14,140 reported to the clinic, and it was found that "he was not altogether recovered, but discharged from the clinic since parole period expired within a few days of visit to clinic." A few months later, the patient was readmitted to the hospital.

The report in No. 13,936 reads, "Discharged at the end of parole period though should ordinarily be continued under care."

In the case of No. 13,738 the record shows that after his discharge from the state hospital, the patient came to the clinic once and was not followed up. Also, the record of the first and only visit reads that "Owing to his poor English he (the patient) did not appear to understand the advice of the examiner." Some months later this patient was readmitted to the hospital.

It is needless to point out the implications of the problem as brought out by citing the above cases, which were taken at random and are typical of much of the work in the clinics at the present time. It should not be gathered that nothing at all is done, for out of a considerable number of patients paroled from one of the hospitals, the writer found that practically every patient who had been paroled reported to the clinic and was seen by the physician at least once during the six months parole period. This in itself was of value, though the general criticism of the work as a whole is that not sufficient is now being done by the state for paroled patients and such as come to the clinics for advice. The social workers are able in a number of cases to assist the patients in placing themselves in positions and in otherwise serving them. As has already been pointed out, however, it is impossible for one worker to follow up paroled and discharged patients from any one of the large state hospitals, and so to serve them and their families that the maximum amount of service will be rendered to these unfortunates. This would involve a large expenditure of money in a kind of service which the state is not prepared to render. The only funds that the state hospitals are empowered to give directly to the patients or their relatives are provided for in the following section of the Insanity Law:[1]

> No patient shall be discharged or paroled from a state hospital without suitable clothing adapted to the season in which he is discharged or paroled; and if it can not be otherwise obtained, the steward shall, upon the order of the superintendent, furnish the same, and money not exceeding twenty-five dollars, to defray his necessary expenses until he can reach his relatives or friends, or find employment to earn a subsistence.

In only a few of the cases discharged or paroled is any money granted to tide the patients over until they find employment. Beyond that and the clinic work the state is not at present supplying any further mental hygiene service to discharged or paroled patients or others in need of such service, the term "mental hygiene service" being used in its broadest sense.

VIII. PAROLED AND DISCHARGED PATIENTS

Mention has already been made of the four-fold division into which the patients have been classified for the purpose of surveying the results of state hospital care and treatment. Regarding the first group, made up of those still in the state hospitals and without dependents or family responsibilities, it is seemingly obvious that very little, if anything, could be accomplished by a detailed study of the families of these persons, more especially from the point of view of their social needs and requirements. It would be possible to unearth facts relative to the heredity, behavior prior to com-

[1] Chap. 27 *of the Consolidated Laws*, Sect. 95.

mitment, industrial history, *etc.*,of the patients. To obtain information of scientific value, it would be necessary to presuppose sufficient knowledge and power of observation and interpretation of given facts on the part of relatives and friends, matters in which large numbers have been found woefully lacking. This is so marked that little value can be attached to statements obtained along these lines from relatives of many of the patients.

In the second group are classified patients who prior to admission to a state hospital had certain family responsibilities, and at the end of one year were still confined in the institutions. The commitment of such persons involved family readjustments of one kind or another, which have already been dwelt upon.

(a) *Details of Survey Form.* The last group contains all those patients discharged or paroled from the state hospitals within a year after admission, and who were permitted to leave the hospitals on parole for six months. In order to study this group carefully it was found to be both advisable and necessary to devise and draw up a form that would serve as the basis for the social investigation, and as a questionuaire and guide to the investigator. Aside from this, it was proposed to obtain as much reliable information as possible regarding the important aspects of the life of the patient after leaving the institution. The form was therefore divided into four main headings, namely, (a) mental, (b) medical or physical, (c) social, and (d) recreational. The thought was that this kind of division would cover all the important factors regarding the lives of the patients and would at the same time bring out the facts relative to our present inadequacies in providing and caring for the mentally sick.

Under *Mental,* the aim was to ascertain the condition of the patient at least a year after discharge, the result of the hospital treatment, after-care or mental hygiene clinic attended, and needs unfulfilled or not being met by the community.

The effect of the medical or physical condition of a person upon his mental well-being is so thoroughly recognized that it needs but little further elucidation. This is particularly true of persons who have been so ill mentally that their commitment to a state hospital or other institution has been found necessary. A discharged or paroled mental case with any one of a large number of serious or troublesome physical ailments will have his ultimate recovery or improvement seriously retarded or even prevented unless such physical difficulty receives timely and expert attention. It might properly be expected that most if not all remediable physical ailments be attended to while the patient is still in the state hospital, or, at least just prior to his parole; and if not then, through the help of the after-care workers, by whom patients can be taken to general hospitals. Because of the overcrowded conditions in the state hospitals any attempt adequately to care for the physical ailments of the patients would result in a state of congestion that would be intolerable. The result is that but little can be attempted in the way of giving patients the attention they actually require if their recovery is to be expedited and the possibility of a relapse eliminated as far as possible.

In a survey of this kind more definite and accurate information can be obtained regarding the social conditions than of either the mental or physical status. Under the classification *Social,* the aim is to determine the condition and progress of the discharged patient, his relationship to his family, the needs of the family group, and what the community has done or is doing to help the family meet these needs. Some might question the necessity and advisability of conducting such an inquiry, presumably assuming that the two problems, state hospital care and family readjustment are separate and distinct problems and not to be considered in conjunction with each other. To such, it is apropos to indicate that worry over lack of employment or even failure to be placed in a suitable position, family and financial difficulties, and innumerable other conditions that arise in family or group life influence mental health, more especially in the cases of those prone to mental disease. The mere fact that a patient has been discharged from a state hospital in an improved or much improved, or even recovered condition, all of these being relative terms only, does not assure him that when he returns to his family and reenters industry he will progress as any normal individual might reasonably expect to after a short or prolonged vacation, or even after residence in a general hospital. The safer assumption is that he will need guidance and advice, and probably financial or other assistance for some time after leaving the institution.

A matter too frequently ignored in considering the needs of mental cases is the important part that suitable forms of recreation can be made to play in facilitating the improvement and recovery of those who are or have been mentally ill. It is because of this that one of the main divisions of the questionnaire deals with the recreation of the discharged and paroled patients. Included under this heading are kinds of recreation sought; result of participation in recreational activities, such as the improvement in sociability, *etc.;* and also, recreational needs unfulfilled, either because the patient does not himself understand the value of proper recreation in the upbuilding and maintenance of health, or because of the lack of recreational facilities in the neighborhood in which the patient lives.

IX. SURVEY OF PAROLED AND DISCHARGED PATIENTS

The investigation of a comparatively large number of patients paroled and discharged from state hospitals involves difficulties not usually met with in surveys concerned with other groups of persons. There are several reasons for this. Patients are at times brought to psychopathic wards of general hospitals from places other than their homes, and, due to their mental condition, their names and more often their correct addresses cannot be obtained. During their stay in a state hospital from which they are subsequently paroled or discharged, it frequently happens that no correct address is ascertained, even though the social workers of the state hospitals aim to get in touch with the friends or relatives of all patients prior to their departure from the institutions. Many patients have no family or other ties in the city and they are consequently lost track of once they are discharged from the hospitals, unless they return to the clinics or to the hospitals following another attack.

It was found furthermore, that a number of families moved away shortly after a member of the family was committed to a state hospital for the insane, and all attempts to locate them were, as a rule, unsuccessful. Partly responsible for this was the circumstance that in making this survey the paroled and discharged cases were not followed up for a year or more after they left the different hospitals. As previously outlined, this lapse of time was permitted in order that after-care workers of the state hospitals might do what they could for the patients, and that they themselves might have time for readjustment before a valuation of the effectiveness of these methods was undertaken. During this time many patients, probably not wishing to return to the neighborhood in which they had been known as queer or "crazy," removed without leaving a forwarding address or telling their neighbors their new place of residence. Other patients left the city or state and facts relative to their condition could not be obtained, All in all, approximately thirty per cent of the paroled and discharged patients were lost track of for the reasons given above, and the observations that follow are based upon the remaining seventy per cent, a sufficiently large number to provide an adequate and satisfactory picture.

X. MENTAL CONDITION

Table 24 shows that of the 784 patients committed to the Manhattan and Central Islip State Hospitals, 285 were discharged within a year after admission as recovered. improved or unimproved. As already indicated, approximately 30 per cent or 85 of the discharged patients could not be located when the attempt was made to follow them up. Of the remaining 200 patients, 20 per cent were found to have fully recovered, practically all of them having originally been diagnosed as cases of manic depressive insanity; 28 per cent showed much improvement, these also largely representing cases of manic depressive insanity; 19 per cent, composed mainly of cases of dementia praecox, showed some slight improvement; 8 per cent showed no improvement whatsoever; 20 per cent returned to the state hospitals within the year; and 5 per cent died within a year after discharge.

From these facts it would seem that about 50 per cent of the paroled and discharged patients were able to return to their former environment and occupations, with the chances in their favor of a future normal life. A question might well be asked at this point as to how many patients of the other 50 per cent might have improved sufficiently to have made it unnecessary for them either to return to the state hospitals for further care, or to remain at home in partial or total idleness, had there been an adequate follow-up system to help them and other patients with advice and personal service. It is of course impossible to answer the question definitely at this time, though we know enough of the value and possibilities of social service in the field of mental hygiene to feel convinced that the state would have saved much eventually had mental hygiene work been established on a broad and comprehensive scale.

Many of the paroled patients who report to the state hospital clinics seemingly do so out of fear that they will be returned to the hospitals unless they come to advise with the doctors regarding their condition during the six months for which they are paroled. In the end it is probably a good thing that they feel a compulsion to seek advice, particularly since most of the paroled patients are kindly disposed towards the doctors and nurses, realizing as they do that a genuine service has been rendered them and their families during a period of severe illness. Should the Jewish patients find themselves in need of further medical advice and treatment after their parole period has expired, they do not often go to the state hospital clinics, where their language is not sufficiently understood and their peculiar psychology is not grasped. They go rather to their family or lodge doctors who are not competent to advise them; or, in some instances, to well-known and thoroughly reliable psychiatrists; or to the mental hygiene clinics maintained by the Free Synagogue, where psychiatrists of established reputations and nurses and social workers trained in mental hygiene work are prepared to assist them socially, financially and otherwise.

In the questionnaire used, when asking the questions "Are needs for mental treatment being met," and "Any further provision for mental treatment needed," the idea was to learn wherein present facilities were inadequate and in need of being strengthened and augmented. The statements already made regarding the shortcomings of our present provisions for the treatment of paroled and discharged patients were fully verified as a result of the study of these patients and their needs. Plans for the development of a constructive program to meet the situation will be presented in a following chapter.

XI. PHYSICAL CONDITION

There are few bodily diseases but what are accompanied by changes more or less severe in the mental condition of the persons affected. Consequently, a person affected mentally and at the same time suffering from some physical ailment, will stand a better chance of regaining his mental health, at least in certain types of cases, if the physical ailment is properly attended to without undue delay. These are fairly well-established facts and account for the questions asked of paroled and discharged patients regarding their physical condition.

It is almost needless to remark that in making the survey it was not feasible to give each paroled and discharged patient a physical examination. Dependence had to be placed in almost every case on what was learned regarding the physical condition of the patient while detained in the psychopathic wards of Bellevue Hospital, and on such other information as could be obtained from a reading of the case records in the state hospitals, the parole records in the clinics, and from the relatives and patients themselves after their discharge from the institutions. Despite all these sources of information, it was not possible to obtain much reliable data regarding the physical condition of the majority of the patients considered. It is easy to understand why this should be so. The psychopathic services of Bellevue and other hospitals are at present primarily concerned with deciding whether or not a given patient is insane and should be committed to a state hospital. The law allows only ten days in which to determine this fact, and does not take into consideration the advisability of thorough physical examinations and treatment in a general hospital or one similarly equipped, of mental cases suffering from physical ailments.

The medical staffs of the state hospitals are trained in the diagnosis and treatment, such as it can be under present overcrowded conditions, of mental diseases; and, while they are quite competent to treat minor physical ailments, it does not need much explanation to make it obvious that they cannot in all fairness be expected to be specialists in all branches of medicine.

Specialists are occasionally consulted for a few of the patients, but this seems to be the exception rather than the rule. To cite just an instance: a former university teacher is a patient in one of the state hospitals in the metropolitan district. He has been diagnosed as a case of dementia praecox of two or more years standing, but despite that his mind is still quite alert. He is also a sufferer from a severe eye affection which seems to aggravate his mental condition. For many weeks he had asked that an eye specialist be called in to advise him as to whether or not he should wear shaded or other glasses, for which he was able and willing to pay. The physician on the ward explained that the patient would have to wait until a member of the board of managers of the hospital, who was at the same time an eye specialist, could find the time to visit him.

Experience in mental hygiene clinics covering a period of years has shown conclusively the need of thorough physical examinations and of the early treatment of the many minor and major illnesses from which a considerable number of persons suffer. The need for this kind of service is greater in mental cases; and, with adequate facilities, no person coming under the care of the state hospitals should be paroled before his physical ailments have been attended to.

At least, no patient should be discharged from parole until the clinic physicians and nurses have seen to it that he has been put in touch with a dispensary or hospital where his physical needs will be properly looked after.

XII. SOCIAL CONDITION

The responsibility of the community to care and provide for its sick members is well recognized by all, and acted upon according to the standards prevailing in different sections of the country. One of the aims of the survey was to learn what the community does through its various social agencies to maintain in health those who have been mentally ill and to prevent their relapse. In order to get at the facts in this matter, the following questions were asked of paroled and discharged patients: present occupation and earnings; regularity of employment since leaving the hospital; reasons, if any, for non-employment; assistance being rendered to patient by any agency, with name of agency and nature of service; assistance rendered to family of patient while latter was in the hospital; and social needs of the family and the patient not being met.

(a) *Employment of Paroled Patients.* In considering the question of employment, the patients must quite naturally be divided into males and females, particularly as far as the adults are concerned, for nearly all the married women resumed their former household tasks of caring for their homes and families. Some of the unmarried young women found it more advisable to remain at home and help in caring for it, than to return to the office or factory in which had formerly been employed. In such instances the change seemed to have quite a salutary effect and helped materially in the improvement of the patient, both physically and mentally. On the whole, the majority of the patients returned to the trades and occupations in which they had been engaged prior to their commitment, for their absence from industry for a period of months made it necessary that they begin to earn money at the earliest possible time. This does not mean that they were all placed shortly after being paroled or discharged, for it must be remembered that many were formerly engaged in seasonal occupations, and if they left the hospital during the slack season it was difficult if not impossible for them to obtain work. On the other hand, if they happened to leave the institution during the busy season and at once returned to the shops and factories with the desire to make up the lost earnings, their health was often adversely affected.

Most of those who returned to their former occupations in industry were cases of manic depressive insanity, and they frequently found it impossible to continue regularly at their trades because they had not fully recovered and could not stand the strain. Others could not work at all as they had been ill since their discharge from the hospital, remaining at home and subsisting on the bounty of friends and relatives. This was true of practically all cases of dementia praecox, most of them working occasionally only and for short periods of time. There were some among these cases who became so discouraged because of their inability to retain a position that they finally gave up trying to find work and remained at home altogether, in some instances developing anti-social habits of conduct. A few of the recovered and much improved cases of manic depressive insanity established themselves in small retail businesses, and seemingly prospered both mentally and financially.

Concerning the earnings of discharged patients, from what has already been said regarding the non-regularity of employment, it is seen that there must have been, as there was, a decrease in the earning power. This entailed in a number of instances a severe financial loss to the families concerned, though it might have been avoided had there existed a social agency, either as an adjunct to state hospitals or otherwise, to obtain suitable employment for such as could not readily find it of their own accord.

(b) *Financial Relief to Families of Patients.* The number of cases that had to be referred to a relief agency were not very large. Several families in which the father and wage-earner had been ill for a considerable time were already known to the United Hebrew Charities, the Jewish relief organization, and it was merely a question of referring the family for further financial assistance until the patient was discharged from the hospital and was able to reenter industry. Other families, unknown to any relief society, had to be taken under care while the wage-earner was confined in a hospital. Usually the relief given was either a subsidy to make up for an insufficient family income, or, where there were no wage-earners or relatives to call upon, the relief agency had to assume the full financial responsibility as best it could. Due to the understandable hesitancy on the part of recipients of financial relief to disclose the extent of the aid given them by the United Hebrew Charities, it was often impossible to obtain accurate facts concerning the amount of relief granted in particular cases. In the year 1919 the United Hebrew Charities spent on families of the insane 4 per cent or $12,400 of its total expenditure for relief. Of recent years there has been some agitation carried on to make the provisions of the law granting a pension to fatherless children who remain at home under the care of their mothers, applicable also to children whose fathers have been committed to a state hospital for the insane. Under the provisions of Chapter 700, Laws of 1920, the Legislature of New York provided that " a board of child welfare may in its discretion, grant an allowance to any dependent mother whose hubsand is an inmate in a state institution for the insane." This law became effective July 1, 1920.

(c) *Dependent Children Committed to Orphan Asylums.* Aside from the problem of financial relief of families in distress, there was the question of the disposition of minor children. The difficulty was most acute when the mother of young children was committed to a state hospital. The social service department in Bellevue Hospital helped to provide for and refer to proper agencies most of the children in need of being placed. Some of the ways used to dispose of such children properly are herewith enumerated, different methods having been found necessary in different circumstances. Children were boarded together with the father during the illness of the mother and until her discharge from the hospital; children were committed to the Hebrew Orphan Asylum, the Hebrew Sheltering Guardian Society and the Hebrew Infant Asylum, through the Department of Public Charities (now the Department of Public Welfare); the father paid neighbors to care for the children; boarding homes were found for the children, the father paying for their care; and children were taken in by relatives. The records of the Hebrew Orphan Asylum indicate that out of approximately 1,200 children, 12 per cent have been committed there because of insanity on the part of either parent; at the Hebrew Sheltering Guardian Society, with a population of about 525 children the percentage is 5.1; while of 350 infants at the Hebrew Infant Asylum 11.5 per cent are there because of insanity in one or both parents.

In presenting the above facts regarding the social condition of paroled and discharged patients, the attempt has been merely to indicate what some of the problems are that beset families in which insanity overthrows the social or economic stability of the group. It was not intended that a detailed social study should be made of all the families concerned, for such a task would not only require a great deal of space, but would also prove quite valueless, as practically all the salient points involved have already been brought out and mentioned. In the following chapter, in which individuals and families are studied in greater detail, the methods employed to meet the mental, physical, social and recreational problems that arise in families in which there is an insane person, are discussed at greater length.

XIII. RECREATIONAL OPPORTUNITIES

Very few, if any, of the patients and their relatives who were interviewed in making this study, realized the important part that proper forms of recreation could be made to play in the improvement and recovery of patients considered sufficiently well to be returned to their former environment. The attempt was made to obtain the facts pertaining to this particular phase of the problem as a whole by asking the following questions: What is being done to provide recreation for the patient; how does the patient spend his spare time; is there any improvement in the sociability of the patient since discharge from the hospital; what agency, if any, is helping the patient to readjust himself along recreational lines, and how; what needs for recreation are not being met. As a matter of fact, it was hardly worth while to ask any but the last question, for in nearly every instance there was a total lack of understanding and appreciation of the therapeutic value of proper forms of recreation. It was furthermore found that the needs of the patients were not being met, and that no agency was interested in helping such patients to grapple with their specific problems. Of the four divisions, namely, the mental, physical, social and recreational, the latter was discovered to be the most neglected field of service, one in which no effort was expended to help the patient.

The shortcomings of our present method of caring for the insane both within and without institutional walls have been more fully illustrated by the facts presented in this chapter. From what has preceded as well as from these facts, it has become apparent that certain adjuncts to the present state hospital system will have to be developed, ere it can be expected that persons adjudged insane and committed to state hospitals for the insane will receive the service and attention that they and their families require in order to return those mentally ill to normal society and to normal ways of living at the earliest possible time.

CHAPTER V

Social Treatment of the Insane

I. INTRODUCTION

Grotius is reputed to have stated that "the care of the human mind is the noblest branch of medicine." Since his day we have come to realize that the care of the human mind, or rather of the insane and borderline cases of insanity, is not altogether a problem for the physician alone, but that other agents and forces in the community must either be called upon or brought into being in order to assist the medical men to meet this problem. This becomes apparent when considering the routine through which the average person who becomes mentally ill passes during the period of his illness.

Whenever a person becomes irrational, markedly depressed or excited, or shows anti-social tendencies which have their roots in the mental state of the individual, the immediate friends and relatives are quite likely to assume that some form of hospital care and treatment is needed. Usually the advice of the family physician is sought, and acting upon his suggestion or that of the police who are called in, the patient is transferred to the psychopathic ward of the general hospital in the community. Once there the patient is subjected to a mental examination and observation of his actions. If, at the end of a few days, a positive diagnosis is made and the patient is found to be insane in the legal sense of the word, he is committed to a state hospital were he remains until it is found advisable to parole or discharge him; or if suffering from a chronic disease, until he dies, unless previously removed by relatives or others. Prior to leaving the state hospital the patient is given a parole card and instructed to report to the clinic or out-patient department of the hospital for further oberva-tion and advice. The work of these clinics has already been summarized and nothing further need be added at this point. However, referring the patient to the clinic and advising him when he reports is to all intents and purposes the last step the state takes. The fact stands out that something further should and must be done if the insane and borderline cases of insanity in the community are to be properly and adequately served.

(a) *Development of Mental Hygiene Movement.* The initiation of the mental hygiene movement, at least insofar as it concerned the organization of state and national societies for the dissemination of facts gathered through surveys and original studies, was largely due to the publication of the autobiography, "A Mind That Found Itself," of Clifford W. Beers, who, since its organization in 1909, has been the secretary of the National Committee for Mental Hygiene. It is undoubtedly true that the publication of this very interesting and well-nigh epoch-making volume came at a time when certain groups in the community were giving much thought to the general problem of the insane, and that Mr. Beers' book served to crystallize opinion and helped to bring together those who shortly thereafter became the founders of the National Committee for Mental Hygiene.

The organization of this group followed closely the movement for the establishment of hospital social service departments in all general hospitals. Dr. Richard C. Cabot of Boston organized the first medical social service department in this country, when in 1905 he developed a social service division in the out-patient department of the Massachusetts General Hospital. The reasons for the organization of this new branch of work were that the physician treating a patient could become acquainted with only certain phases of the mental and physical condition of the patient, and that it was necessary to call in the trained social service worker to assist the physician in making a more accurate diagnosis and in rendering the prescribed treatment more effective. This new form of service was at first designed primarily for those who came to the out-patient department of the general hospital. Since then the movement has spread to practically all the large general hospitals in the country, and the social service departments now serve both the ward and dispensary patients. The state hospitals for the insane in New York, following the development of the hospital social service idea, appointed social service workers to follow-up as many patients as they could, to assist at the clinics, and to obtain such additional information regarding particular patients as was found necessary by the attending physicians.

To those who became interested in the better care of the insane, it early became evident that the service rendered by the state to patients lacked one very essential element, and that was proper mental hygiene care. Organized work in mental hygiene may be described in various ways, depending upon one's viewpoint and special interest.[1] The viewpoint expressed here is not that of the physician but rather that of the layman, interested in according to mental cases that kind of service which had its origin in medical social service, but which has during the past decade developed its own methods of work and means of serving. The state

[1] Beers, C. W., "Organized Work in Mental Hygiene," *Mental Hygiene,*" Jan., 1917, p. 81.

hospitals, due to financial and legal difficulties, have stopped virtually at the point at which the hospital social service movement began, and it has been left to private organizations to develop the technique of rendering mental hygiene service.

II. ORGANIZATION AND DEVELOPMENT OF A MENTAL HYGIENE AGENCY

Following closely the organization of a social service department by Dr. Cabot in Boston, a group of public spirited men and women helped to organize such a department in Bellevue Hospital, New York City, by providing the funds with which to carry on certain very important phases of the work for which the city did not and could not appropriate money. Because of the very large number of patients admitted to the hospital, as well as treated in the out-patient departments, the problem of supplying adequate social service to all groups of patients presented difficulties, some of which have not as yet been surmounted. It should be noted that to Bellevue Hospital come patients from practically all parts of the greater city; and that, besides its general wards for medical and surgical cases, it also has a psychopathic department which handles approximately 6,000 patients a year. Receiving such a large number of patients, it is apparent that many races and nationalities are represented in the lists of admissions.

Bellevue Hospital necessarily admits a rather large number of Jewish patients annually, for though the Jews of New York have organized and maintain several general hospitals to which Jews largely seek admission, nevertheless the number of beds is quite insufficient to accommodate all who want treatment in the semi-private Jewish institutions. In order to serve beween 5,000 and 6,000 Jewish patients who are admitted to Bellevue Hospital annually, and of whom about 1,100 come to the psychopathic wards, a Jewish agency, namely the social service department of the Free Synagogue, has undertaken to serve particularly the Jewish patients, most of whom feel out of place in an institution in which the Mosaic dietary laws are not observed and in which their language, when not English, is not understood and their own distinctive psychology not fully grasped.

With the development of the work, the realization that the psychopathic cases demanded a different kind of service became apparent. It was found, for instance, that the resident psychiatrists often believed that certain cases could recover outside of a state hospital more readily than they could within the walls of such an institution; and yet, they did not feel safe in sending such patients back to their own homes, in which the mental difficulty had developed and to relatives who did not understand the nature of the ailment or the proper care of the patient. Since approximately 71 per cent of the patients admitted to the psychopathic wards were committed to a state hospital, the social service department was often called upon to advise the family and help, financially and otherwise, in their readjustment to new social conditions until the father or mother or other member of the family was discharged from the state hospital. A further phenomenon also aroused interest in the need for a special division to care for mental cases, and that was the considerable number of patients readmitted from year to year.

It was these facts, as well as the realization, through daily contact with psychopathic cases and their problems, of the shortcomings of the provisions made by the state and city officially, and by the community as a whole, that prompted the organization of a mental hygiene division as a part of the social service department of the Free Synagogue.[1] The series of steps in the development of this particular mental hygiene agency is probably more or less typical of the way in which other similar agencies have and will come into being, unless through propaganda and widespread education, various communities can be made to realize the duty they owe to the mentally sick in their midst.

III. ACTIVITIES OF A MENTAL HYGIENE AGENCY

Stating the matter briefly, the chief purposes of any society or committee for mental hygiene are: conservation of mental health; prevention of nervous and mental disorders and mental deficiency; and improvement in the care and treatment of those suffering from any of these disorders. Though methods of work and the amount of attention given to some activities vary, practically all societies for mental hygiene are seeking to achieve their aims in the following ways: (a) by means of campaigns of education; (b) through social service activities; (c) by surveys and special studies; (d) by influencing the enactment of proper and necessary legislation; (e) by cooperating with other agencies to achieve better results in the care and treatment of mental cases.

Several of the above items in a mental hygiene program explain themselves and need no further elaboration. The matter of social service activities, however, presents a definite problem which has many ramifications. To begin with, there is the question of the organization and the personnel of the clinic to which the patients taken under care are referred. The usual organization requires that there be a physician trained in psychiatry, a mental hygiene or psychiatric social worker, and a stenographic secretary.

[1] State Hosp. Comm., *25th Annual Report*, p. 451.

Having carefully selected the staff for each clinic, it becomes necessary to determine upon the scope of work which the agency operating the clinics deems it can successfully carry through. The two clinics maintained by the social service department of the Free Synagogue at a cost of about $6,000 per year for each clinic, aim to render the following services to all those who are referred to them by various individuals and social agencies in the community:

1. To treat psychoneuroses and all so-called borderline cases of mental diseases in adults and children.
2. To inform the wage earners and others truthfully about conditions for the care of the insane in the state hospitals, to explain the significance of commitment to them and to assist them in committing proper cases to the state hospitals as well as to private sanatoria, suitable to the needs of the patients and the means of the family.
3. To make careful individual study of each case by keeping in close touch with the individual and his surroundings.
4. To arrange for the social care of both patient and family whenever social needs appear.
5. To facilitate the convalescent care of patients in need of this service, especially of those discharged from institutions.
6. To assist convalescents and others in obtaining suitable employment and to aid in readjusting them to their environment.

To carry out the program as outlined above, it becomes necessary to call for the cooperation of various agencies in the community, such as orphan asylums, child-placing institutions, relief organizations, convalescent homes, general and special hospitals for the treatment of physical ailments, employment agencies, and a number of others, all of which have been found to be essentials in properly caring for mental hygiene cases. The Free Synagogue clinics and those associated in their work, do what they themselves can in providing for the mental, physical, social and recreational needs of the patient and the family of which he or she is a part. The cooperation and help of other agencies is sought whenever it is felt that the patient or the family is in need of such additional service as the mental hygiene agency is not as yet prepared to render, or as is altogether and properly the function of another type of agency.

IV. TYPICAL CASES OF A MENTAL HYGIENE AGENCY

The kind of cases that are referred to a mental hygiene agency are naturally of many sorts and include practically all varieties and classifications. In the activities of such an agency, decision must be made at an early period as to the kinds of patients that can be more or less successfully treated and served, and as to which categories must be referred to other agencies and institutions. Thus, it has been found in the clinics mentioned that all mental defectives must be referred to other organizations, as the attempt is to deal only with such cases as present definite psychoses or neuroses, or a borderline condition of either of these groups of ailments. In the pages that follow, typical cases that have been referred to and served by a mental hygiene agency over a period of years will be presented in outline form. Because of the fact that certain types of patients predominate not only in the psychopathic wards and in the state hospitals, but also in the mental hygiene clinics as well, several cases will be presented under certain headings and only one or two under such classifications as appear less frequently in the admissions to hospitals and clinics.

A word should be said regarding the outline according to

which the study of the cases was made. Following the usual order adhered to in state hospitals for the insane, the diagnosis is presented first; then follows as much of the family history regarding insanity in the family as has been ascertained; the personal history of the patient; and a statement regarding the onset of the psychosis. This ends the first divison of the outline. In the second part or division, is presented the method pursued by the mental hygiene agency in attempting to serve the patient and his family, and the work done to meet or help solve the mental, physical, social and recreational problems of the patient and his dependents. Finally, the result of the care bestowed upon the patient and his family by the mental hygiene agency and the other organizations and institutions whose services had to be called upon, is stated in a thoroughly unbiased way.

V. CASE STUDIES

MANIC DEPRESSIVE INSANITY

Case 1

Diagnosis. Manic depressive insanity, depressed type, with psychoneurotic symptoms.

Family History. Sister of patient in a state hospital for five years with a diagnosis of dementia praecox.

Personal History. Male; age 35; born in Russia; came to United States 21 years ago; clothing operator; has wife and seven minor children.

Onset of Psychosis. A few weeks before coming to the clinic, patient was riding in the subway and suddenly his head began to pain, he felt dizzy and could not go home alone. His whole body shook; could not sleep at night; felt sick and like crying all the time. His condition was worse in the morning than later in the day. Hands felt weak and became easily tired; was depressed; felt as if he had a wound on top of his head. Had feeling of inadequacy. Had been nervous and tormented by peculiar sexual ideas for several years.

Method

Mental. Patient came to clinic a number of times within a few months, but showed no improvement. Insisted he wanted to enter a state hospital as a voluntary patient as he could not remain at home with his wife and children, for they aggravated his condition. Did not merely want to stay away from home but also to be where his wife could not come to see him regularly and annoy him. Arranged for patient to enter a state hospital on a voluntary commitment. Remained there about nine months, leaving the institution in an improved condition. He returned home to his family and worked for a year as a newsstand attendant. Suddenly left his work and returned as a voluntary patient to the state hospital, where he has remained for about a year. He does not wish to go home as he fears to assume the responsibility of caring for his large family and to live with his wife. Mother of latter died in an insane asylum and daughter is nervous, high-strung, hyper-sexual, and makes unusual sexual demands upon her husband when he is at home. Patient prefers to remain in the state hospital until he has fully recovered; has shown marked improvement and expects to leave the institution within a few months.

Physical. Little was necessary to be done for the patient, except to give him a thorough physical examination and assure him there was nothing wrong with him physically. Looked after the physical conditions of wife and children; provided set of teeth for wife.

Social. Wife of patient insisted that she could not care for seven small children when her husband was away from home, as they made her very nervous. To prevent a breakdown, two children were committed to an orphan asylum. This relieved mother greatly. Family provided with rent, living expenses, clothing, *etc.* during time that patient was and has been in state hospital. Children sent to vacation homes during summer.

Recreational. When out of hospital patient was advised and encouraged to take long walks, to pass spare time in parks, *etc.* Recreation provided for wife and children.

Result

Patient still in state hospital, and is expecting to return home within a few months in a much improved condition. Social service work has aimed properly to care for family while the patient was in hospital, to adjust the family preparatory to his homecoming, and to educate the wife as to what should be her proper attitude towards patient when he returns from the hospital. Frequent visits made to patient in hospital by worker to help him develop a greater sense of responsibility towards his family and a better understanding of his wife.

CASE 2

Diagnosis. Manic depressive insanity.

F. H. Negative.

P. H. Male; age 38; born in Austria; U. S. 18 years; clothing operator; married; wife and five minor children.

Psychosis. For three years patient suffered cramps in abdomen and pains in upper and lower limbs. Following death of sister-in-law became very nervous and upset; could not sleep; imagined he saw the dead woman. Became depressed and quiet. Year and a half before coming to clinic had an attack of manic depressive insanity, lasting for a few days. While at work became excited and mixed up; did not sleep for a few nights. Later complained of pains on top of head, sleeplessness and inability to tolerate any noises. Had suicidal thoughts; occasionally things became dark before his eyes; noises in ears; while at work and away from home imagined some calamity had befallen family.

Method

Mental. Patient reported at clinic every two weeks for several months; later, as mental condition improved, these visits were made every month or two; patient visited regularly at home by mental hygiene worker. Wife of patient developed a sympathetic condition and also had to be treated at clinic. Family under care for three and a half years.

Physical. Examined physically at clinic and advised regarding personal habits, diet, *etc.* Because of complaints regarding cramps and pains in upper and lower limbs, had X-ray taken of stomach; patient found to be suffering from a gastric ulcer, which seemed to be the cause of most of his difficulties. Successful operation performed for an ulcer of lesser curvature of stomach. Sent patient to convalescent home following discharge from hospital. Physical needs of wife and children attended to.

Social. During entire time that patient and his family were under care, supplied family with rent and living expenses whenever patient was unable to work, clothed the entire family, and provided such other things as were needed, as an abdominal belt following operation. Family visited regularly by nurse and mental hygiene worker; provided employment for patient in a model factory, where he could work according to his strength.

Recreational. Patient advised by clinic physician as to kind of recreation best suited to his needs; provided with tickets to high-class concerts.

Result

Patient has fully recovered, both physically and mentally. His wife recovered as soon as symptoms presented by patient disappeared. Patient now earning high wages, has moved family to better and large quarters, and status of entire family has been raised.

Case 3

Diagnosis. Manic depressive insanity.

F. H. Father insane.

P. H. Female; age 27; born in Russia; U. S. 1½ years; housework; married five years; two children.

Psychosis. After birth of second child became melancholy, dejected, could not sleep; spoke sparingly; cried during night; feared fate of father; continually complained of head being mixed-up; attempted suicide by inhaling gas; showed no impairment of memory, but lacked insight into her condition.

Method

Mental. Sent patient to a private sanatorium for four months; came home in an improved condition; following this, she came to clinic regularly for two years where she was examined and advised by physician. Home of patient visited by mental hygiene worker, several times a week immediately after discharge from sanatorium and at regular intervals thereafter.

Physical. Ailments attended to at dispensaries, accompanied by nurse or mental hygiene worker.

Social. Children boarded out while patient was in sanatorium; worker helped patient adjust herself to conditions at home; advised and trained in proper care of children; advised as to care of self, personal habits, household management, *etc.* Case continued for four years.

Recreational. Advised as to proper recreation; walks, outings, *etc.* Taken out for walks by worker.

Result

Became completely readjusted and made full recovery. Had no relapse several years after care had been discontinued.

CASE 4

Diagnosis. Manic depressive insanity, depressed type.

F. H. Unascertained.

P. H. Female; age 27; born in Russia; U. S. 3 years; housework; married; two children.

Psychosis. Suffered a depression caused by fatigue; showed debility; feeling of insufficiency; insomnia; anorexia; unable to do any work or care for self or household. Complained of pains and aches all over body; became easily excited.

Method

Mental. Sent to a private sanatorium but refused to stay there more than two weeks, complaining that the associations there made her feel worse. Brought to clinic regularly, where she was examined, and both she and her husband advised regarding care of patient. Mental hygiene worker visited patient frequently at her home.

Physical. Complaints and ailments attended to at hospitals and dispensaries, accompanied by worker. Needs of children looked after.

Social. Unemployment of husband necessitated supplementing family income and providing clothing. Patient advised and shown how properly to care for self, for children and for home.

Recreational. Advised.

Result

Two years after original attack patient feeling very much improved. No further need to attend clinic and has not had another attack.

CASE 5

Diagnosis. Manic depressive insanity, circular type.

F. H. Mother insane; maternal aunt in state hospital for the insane.

P. H. Male; age 36; born in Austria; U. S. 11 years; carpenter; married; wife and five children.

Psychosis. Patient had been home for one month and was inactive, melancholy, shunned company. At first visit to clinic spoke in a random manner; showed poor orientation as to time; appeared confused; complained of head being mixed up; in a hypomanic state.

Method

Mental. At first examination at clinic psychiatrist recommended commitment to a state hospital and same was arranged by worker. Remained in the hospital for seven weeks. On discharge condition was much improved with prospect of ultimate recovery. Returned to clinic after discharge and found to be in a hypomanic state. Examined and treated at clinic for 16 months, patient coming very regularly. Worker visited patient frequently at his home.

Physical. No physical needs were discovered that needed attention.

Social. Family provided with rent, living expenses, clothing, *etc.* during the time that patient was in the state hospital. Adjusted economically during hospital residence and after discharge. Financial sources of worry and distress removed, as these seemed to be important contributing causes to illness of patient.

Recreational. Advised.

Result

Patient made full recovery; returned to work and earned sufficient property to support self and family. No relapse after several years.

Case 6

Diagnosis. Manic depressive insanity, circular type.

F. H. Unascertained.

P. H. Female; age 28; born in Roumania; U. S. 15 years; housework; married; husband and four children.

Psychosis. Patient admitted to psychopathic ward in depressed, irritable, hyperactive condition. Husband refused to sign commitment papers; patient discharged to his custody in hypomanic state. Similar attack five years previous following confinement. In a few days husband returned patient to psychopathic ward; committed; remained five months in state hospital and discharged after showing a slight improvement. Three months later relapsed; returned to state hospital for seven months; discharged improved. Shortly thereafter came to mental hygiene clinic.

Method

Mental. Examined and advised regularly at clinic by physician and at home by worker. Examined regularly and watched carefully for several months prior to and following last confinement.

Physical. Arranged for confinement; needs of patient and children attended to at clinic and dispensaries.

Social. Cared for children in a boarding home following discharge of patient from state hospital, when patient first came under care of mental hygiene agency. Source of stress thus removed for a period of several months, during which time patient recuperated. Husband enabled to obtain better and more lucrative employment. Family moved into better quarters, this resulting in improvement of all members of family.

Recreational. Advised and helped to carry out plans.

Result

Patient made full recovery and suffered no relapse within two years after last confinement.

CASE 7

Diagnosis. Allied to manic depressive insanity.

F. H. Negative.

P. H. Female; age 19; born in Russia; U. S. 2 years; operator; single.

Psychosis. Two months prior to admission to psychopathic ward patient became weak and fainted. Remained in bed; did not speak; stated she was weak and could not work; at times cried; no hallucinations; no delusions; showed some depression and irritability. Cause of illness as stated by relatives was that a younger sister married a man with whom patient was in love.

Method

Mental. Patient was taken from the psychopathic ward and sent to a private sanatorium where she remained for four weeks. Left before making a full recovery, refusing to remain among "crazy" people. Afterwards was brought to clinic regularly, examined and advised. Home frequently visited by worker.

Physical. Advised at clinic regarding constipation and cardiac palpitation.

Social. Assisted financially; interested in a settlement class.

Recreational. Stimulated interest in theatres and social affairs.

Result

Patient improved rapidly and soon returned to former employment. Feeling well two years after being discharged from further supervision and care. Patient became adjusted to home conditions, as well as to life in a metropolis.

Case 8

Diagnosis. Allied to manic depressive insanity.

F. H. Negative.

P. H. Female; age 42; born in Roumania; U. S. 10 years; housework; husband and five children.

Psychosis. At first visit to clinic, patient complained of insomnia; was excitable; accused husband of going out with other women; no basis for this complaint. Also accused her mother of personal antagonism. Could not do housework; showed no interest in her children. Threatened to commit suicide on several occasions. About ten similar attacks in fifteen years.

Method

Mental. Patient induced to come to clinic regularly where physician examined and advised her. Worker at first visited the patient several times a week and helped her to make necessary mental adjustments. Later, as she showed improvement, she was visited at regular intervals and stimulated to take a wider interest in her home and family.

Physical. Examined at clinic and advised.

Social. Patient was very unsystematic in her household work, and since her marriage had never learned how properly to care for home and children. Regular and frequent visits of worker who taught her these things helped materially. Attended to needs of children.

Recreational. Could only advise. Had not learned nor ever appreciated the value of proper kind of recreation.

Result

Patient had improved very much when supervision was ended. Has continued at this level for a number of years, and stated that the mental hygiene agency has aided her more properly to understand herself.

Case 9

Diagnosis. Allied to manic depressive insanity.

F. H. Negative.

P. H. Female; age 14; born in U. S.; public school pupil.

Psychosis. Following the extraction of some teeth, patient became somewhat confused; remained in bed for a month, after which she showed a little improvement. Within a month again became confused, irritable, talked of people following her about and speaking ill of her; very fidgety; shortly thereafter could not talk nor use hands. Parents brought her to psychopathic ward and in a few days she was committed and sent to a state hospital, where she remained for three weeks and discharged in an improved condition.

Method

Mental. After discharge from state hospital was brought to clinic and examined by physician. Patient found to have improved very much and return to school advised. Came to clinic several times, being examined and advised. Visited frequently by worker.

Physical. Sent to summer camp for adolescent girls maintained by agency; remained there several weeks until she was in good physical condition.

Social. Family moved to better neighborhood; parents were aged and did not understand the patient and her needs. Worker helped to adjust the patient to her parents and to give them another point of view regarding their daughter. By visiting school teachers, worker brought about a better understanding of patient by teachers.

Recreational. Patient taken to a settlement and interested in a club and in other activities.

Result

Patient improved very much physically; recovered mentally; no relapse within two years after being taken under care.

DEMENTIA PRAECOX

CASE 10

Diagnosis. Dementia praecox, simple.

F. H. Negative, except for a brother who is nervous and very irritable.

P. H. Male; age 24; born in Russia; U. S. 18 years; graduated public school at 14 years; attended evening high school two years; clerical worker, helper in restaurants, odd jobs; single.

Psychosis. Patient first complained of being ill five years before coming to clinic; had many jobs since then but could not hold one for any length of time, being either discharged or leaving of own accord. At first visit to clinic, complained of inability to get along with people, because they passed remarks about him indirectly; attitude and manner somewhat constrained; gave expression to peculiar ideas and in discussing his condition became quite rambling and involved; somewhat evasive in answering questions and expressed delusional ideas of an absurd character. Also referred to some sexual ideas.

Method

Mental. Given general advice as to hygiene of mind during visits to clinics. Frequent and lengthy discussions and talks with psychiatrist and social worker seemed to have a salutary effect upon patient; always left the clinic in a better and happier frame of mind than when he came.

Physical. Patient suffered from some bladder trouble which rendered him incontinent. Taken by worker to specialists for treatment; also to hospital where patient was kept for about a week. Condition complained of very much improved, though the ailment seemed to have its origin in mental rather than physical condition of patient. Remorse over earlier sexual excesses and masturbation seemingly influenced condition.

Social. Due to mental and physical condition of patient, could not hold any position for a length of time; helped him on a number of occasions to obtain work of a suitable nature, particularly light outdoor work. Did not remain long in any one job, though always managed to earn enough to be self-supporting. Brought about adjustment between patient and his family.

Recreational. Advised and helped patient join classes in gymnasium, for such exercise as would be suitable to his own condition. Advised as to other forms of recreation.

Result

After four years, mental condition of patient has shown no further deterioration, though certain seemingly chronic neurasthenic symptoms persist. Bladder condition somewhat improved. Patient wanders from one city to another, always returning to New York when he is not well and then coming to clinic. This has prevented continuous, constructive work for any length of time.

CASE 11

Diagnosis. Dementia praecox, hebephrenic form.

F. H. Father somewhat peculiar in his actions and highly nervous; mother dull; older brother patient in a state hospital with a diagnosis of dementia praecox, hebephrenic type.

P. H. Male; age 20; born in Russia; U. S. 10 years; did not graduate from public school; helper and odd jobs; single.

Psychosis. Patient complained of as being very lazy; worked at irregular intervals in many different positions since the age of 14 years. Enlisted in army at 18 years and discharged within ten weeks because of mental condition. Acted peculiarly in a restaurant, was arrested, and sent to psychopathic ward for observation. Mother refused to sign commitment papers and patient was discharged to her custody. Very difficult to manage and get along with at home; unruly; threatening bodily violence to members of family.

Method

Mental. After discharge from psychopathic ward, referred to mental hygiene agency. At first visit given thorough mental examination and found to be a badly deteriorated case. Patient expressed desire to enter a state hospital; worker at clinic arranged for his voluntary commitment, as he refused and mother would not accede to a regular commitment through psychopathic ward. Discharged from state hospital at own request at end of ten days. Mother again refused to have him committed, though father was quite willing to have that done. Very troublesome and pugnacious while in state hospital.

Physical. Thorough physical examination at clinic revealed no physical defects needing treatment.

Social. Obtained several positions for patient both in country on a farm and in the city. Had difficulties with fellow workers and employers in every place. Usually discharged within a day. This so discouraged him that he later refused to look for work or report when work was found for him; preferred to loaf in street and around house.

Recreational. Very difficult to advise because of negativistic attitude, as well as hostility to all doctors and mental hygiene workers.

Result

Very little could be accomplished with a patient in this condition. Patient smashed windows with stones in home of head of organization. Next day sent registered letter threatening life of worker unless sum of $2,500 was given by worker to patient within two days. When arrested at his home a heavy slung-shot was found in his pocket. At police station stated he intended to kill worker unless money was given him within specified time. A commission found him insane and he was sent to state hospital for criminally insane. No improvement after one year residence there.

Case 12

Diagnosis. Dementia praecox, hebephrenic form. Constitutional psychopath.

F. H. Negative.

P. H. Male; age 20; born in U. S.; helper in dental office; high school 2 years; single.

Psychosis. Patient always quiet and seclusive; rather studious and never cared to associate with boys. Left high school at age of 16 years, when he complained of being ill and unable further to continue his studies; stated his heart pained him and that he felt a choking sensation in his throat. Since then he became more seclusive, timid, and shunned company of others. Occasionally became excited and would quarrel with sisters. Taken to psychopathic ward by father, where he showed all the above symptoms. Had no delusions or hallucinations, and no suicidal ideas. Father refused to sign commitment papers and took patient home.

Method

Mental. Directly after discharge from psychopathic ward referred to mental hygiene clinic. During period of six years that patient was under care he came to clinic at regular intervals to see physician for examination and advice. Though fearful of all physicians because of having been in psychopathic ward, he developed much confidence in physicians who treated him at clinics, as he came to feel that his condition was understood and received sympathetic consideration. Advised regularly both by physicians and by workers.

Physical. Came to clinic whenever he had some physical ailment that needed attention and could be prescribed for at clinic. Referred and taken to different hospitals and dispensaries whenever need arose.

Social. Patient unable to find work at which he could remain any length of time. Expressed desire to learn a trade, preferably mechanical dentistry; sent to a school, where he became proficient at his work. Organization paid for course and incidental expenses. Aided occasionally with living expenses and clothing. Position as mechanical dentist obtained for him; after becoming proficient able to earn $25.00 per week. Inability to earn more due to shaking of hands. When work in his line was slow, obtained other employment for him.

Recreational. Patient advised by physician and worker as to kind of recreation best suited to his needs. Taken out for walks; interested a college student in him; helped to plan spare-time activities.

Result

For several years patient has been able to take care of self financially; has not found it necessary to return to psychopathic ward nor to enter a state hospital. Is no longer fearful of people, particularly of police as formerly; goes alone to theatres, parks, *etc.* Still nervous but now understands his condition and knows what to do when he is not feeling well, having been advised at clinic.

CASE 13

Diagnosis. Dementia praecox, katatonic form.

F. H. Father in state hospital for insane; diagnosis, organic nervous disease. Paternal aunt committed suicide while depressed.

P. H. Male; age 22; born in U. S.; stock clerk; public school graduate; single.

Psychosis. A few weeks prior to being brought to psychopathic ward patient became quite nervous and gave vent to undue excitement. During the previous election period became engaged in many heated arguments and worked himself into a highly nervous state, resulting in sleeplessness and marked loss of appetite. Also worried about being drafted and became distressed because he feared he was losing his health. Began to hear imaginary voices; became much depressed; could not eat or sleep; refused to speak to anyone, feared to meet strangers. Preferred to sit in a corner or in a room by himself, usually without changing his posture for hours at a time.

Method

Mental. Parents refused to sign commitment papers and took patient home. Then sent him to a private sanatorium for two months where he showed little, if any, improvement. Social worker advised taking patient home, particularly since family had to borrow money to pay for care of patient. Upon return home brought to clinic for examination, but little could be accomplished as patient refused to answer questions of examining physician, and did not speak at all. Worker called at home of patient regularly and after many efforts induced patient to go out for walks with him. This seemed to help very much; parents then had someone take him out daily for long walks in nearby park and to other places about the city. Gradually began to talk, to eat regularly, and to look after clothes, *etc*. Family advised as to how best to get along with patient. In two months latter began to talk to worker and to receive him more cordially than had formerly been the case. At end of four months patient began to speak freely to all, though refusing to account for previous behavior.

Physical. No physical needs discovered that needed attention.

Social. No need, except to advise family regarding commitment of father of patient.

Recreational. Advised.

Result

Patient found work by himself and has continued in one position for nearly two years. Seems fully recovered; earning higher wages than previous to illness; sociability has become normal.

CASE 14

Diagnosis. Dementia praecox, paranoid form.

F. H. Sister acted in a strange and peculiar manner for a number of years; later committed suicide.

P. H. Male; age 43; born in Russia; U. S. 21 years; shoe operator; married; wife and six children.

Psychosis. Patient referred to clinic by another organization. At first clinic examination, talked very profusely and volubly about his domestic difficulties; stated his troubles began when he married, because his wife is smarter than he is; also, that his wife has always been and still is unfaithful; that the youngest child of the family is not his own. Could not tell his story connectedly; stuttered and it was very difficult to follow him; admitted he was very nervous. Troublesome and abusive at home; used vile language to wife and children; threatened bodily harm to wife; very easily influenced by opinions of friends and relatives, to whom he spoke openly of the supposed infidelity of his wife.

Method

Mental. Patient induced to come to clinic after a number of visits to home and much persuasion. Insisted there was nothing the matter with him mentally. Subsequently visited clinic on several occasions; physician and worker helped to straighten out and explain away some of his mental difficulties and doubts, and to bring about a better understanding between patient and his family.

Physical. Arranged for treatment of heart condition of which patient complained; examined at clinic and treatment prescribed for minor ills. Several children and wife suffering with various physical ills; treatment at hospitals arranged for; convalescent care provided for children.

Social. Patient at first did not make sufficient allotment to family out of his earnings. Due to this and difficulty he caused at home, wife agreed to have him summoned to Domestic Relations Court on charge of non-support, as patient would not heed advice given him by worker. Latter went to court with wife, and upon presentation of facts by worker, judge ordered a fifty per cent increase in allowance and also that patient must live away from home. This arrangement helped matters greatly for family; for first time in many years patient made to realize his responsibility to family; begged wife to be permitted to return home, promising to behave, not to accuse her of infidelity, and to give her all his earnings. After several months' absence from home, for sake of smaller children, wife advised to permit patient to come home. Employment obtained for oldest son; family aided with rent, living expenses, clothing, when patient did not or could not provide same for family.

Recreational. No cooperation on part of patient. Preferred to spend spare time at home with children.

Result

One year after patient returned home, conducting self more properly and no longer abuses wife and children. Has acknowledged that baby he formerly disowned, was his own child and that it resembled its paternal grandmother. Family able to support self through earnings of children and contributions of patient. Latter has become readjusted to home and family. Questionable whether he has rid himself of idea that wife was unfaithful.

Case 15

Diagnosis. Allied to dementia praecox.

F. H. Father died from apoplexy; mother died in thirteenth confinement, in convulsions.

P. H. Female; age 21; born in Russia; U. S. 2 years; housework; saleswoman before marriage; child one year old.

Psychosis. Patient developed pneumonia, taken to a general hospital and remained there four weeks. Thence transferred to psychopathic ward. Refused to take food and medication; recognized no one; crawled in bed and hid under covers when anyone came near her; scratched and attempted to bite nurses; sat in bed rocking back and forth, moaning all the while. Depressed and refused to talk, sometimes lying in a very rigid position. Recovered sufficiently within four days to be permitted to go home with husband, who refused to sign commitment papers.

Method

Mental. Family visited shortly after discharge of patient from psychopathic ward. After many visits, patient induced to come to clinic, where she was found to be dull and inactive, manifesting very little initiative. Did not recognize physician, who had also treated her in the psychopathic ward. Several visits a week to home by social worker and regular visits to clinic for examination and advice by physician, helped to stimulate patient to care for home and baby, to become more sociable, *etc.* Patient refused to enter a private sanatorium when worker offered to send her there, as she did not want to leave her child.

Physical. Obtained necessary dental work for patient and agency paid for same. Gave birth to a baby while under care; arranged for necessary care of patient and children.

Social. Husband a house painter with short seasonal employment. Moved family into better and cleaner quarters, near home of an aunt who had promised to help look after patient. Supplied living expenses and rent whenever necessary, clothing, *etc.* Taught patient how to keep her house clean, how properly to prepare and serve meals. Aided brother who lived with patient to enter a trade school and to obtain employment.

Recreational. Advised regarding kind of outdoor exercise to take; worker took patient for walks. Instructed in proper kinds of recreation.

Result

Patient under care for six years. During all this time it was never necessary for her to return to psychopathic ward or to go to any other institution because of mental relapse. Became much brighter, showed more initiative, talked more fluently; in general, learned to take a better view of life, and to exhibit good insight into her condition. Economically adjusted when husband obtained regular employment.

PARANOID CONDITION

CASE 16

Diagnosis. Paranoid condition.

F. H. Unascertained.

P. H. Male; age 56; born in Russia; U. S. 35 years; cashier in restaurant; married second time; first wife died; adult daughter of first marriage; daughter 10 years of second marriage.

Psychosis. Patient became excited while walking in street and brought to psychopathic ward. Stated he worked as night cashier in restaurants for over 25 years; never had any free time; for a number of years he was being followed about; strangers threatened to kill him; called him vile names; pointed him out to others, cursing him and saying, "There he goes—that man is no good." Thought there must be some society interested in ruining and killing him. Later feared to go to work; remained at home and would not even go down stairs to stoop of house, because he believed he was always being watched. Wife refused to sign commitment papers and patient discharged to her custody.

Method

Mental. After discharge from psychopathic ward referred to mental hygiene agency. Came to clinic several times, but would not talk to physician unless social worker left the room, as he feared latter might be a detective or a member of a secret society interested in harming him. Later became convinced this was not so. Very little could be done with patient at clinic as he feared to speak to physician of his troubles.

Physical. Complained of severe rheumatic pains all over body and particularly in legs. Patient very anxious to enter some hospital for treatment, provided he could be convinced that institution to which he would go was not one for the insane. Worker arranged for treatment in a general hospital. Patient left there because of poor food, and decided to remain at home thereafter. Wife of patient complained of various ailments and treatment arranged.

Social. Obtained several light positions for patient; helped family financially. When patient insisted on remaining at home and refused to go out to work because he feared he was being followed, arranged for wife, who could sew, to take work home and to have patient help her.

Recreational. No provision could be made; no cooperation.

Result

Plan of having patient remain at home and help wife has worked out successfully for about two years. No longer so fearful as formerly, due to exciting causes, namely, contact with strangers, having been removed. Family able to get along without financial assistance, though patient has by no means recovered. He has merely been somewhat readjusted.

CASE 17

Diagnosis. Paranoid condition.

F. H. Unascertained.

P. H. Female; age 33; born in Russia; U. S. 14 years; housework; deserted by husband; three minor children.

Psychosis. Patient referred to clinic by hospital social service. Found to have been queer, nervous and quarrelsome since childhood; neglected her children and home. At clinic stated gangsters followed her and called her vile names; had complained to police of supposed persecution by "Black Hand" and others. Moved from place to place to avoid persecutors; suspicious that husband was in league with her enemies.

Method

Mental. Patient had been sent to psychopathic ward by Department of Public Charities, where she had gone to complain of persecution. Relatives refused to sign commitment papers and patient was discharged to their custody. Worker followed-up patient after discharge and succeeded in having her come to clinic, where she repeated her story of persecution. In five months did not come to clinic more than twice; followed by worker from one address to another for period of seven months. No cooperation either in clinic or at home.

Physical. No cooperation.

Social. Helped to have children committed to an orphan asylum after relatives could no longer do anything with patient.

Recreational. No cooperation.

Result

Relatives had patient committed to a state hospital. Mental hygiene agency could not get patient to cooperate in the least.

CASE 18

Diagnosis. Paranoid condition.

F. H. Mother "nervous".

P. H. Male; age 42; born in Austria; U. S. 16 years; clothing presser; married; wife and four children.

Psychosis. Wife had patient arrested for non-support; judge in Domestic Relations Court sent patient to psychopathic ward for observation. Wife stated that patient was always of an obstinate disposition but showed no definite mental symptoms until about one year previous to hospital admission. Then began to complain of various pains over his entire body; worked very irregularly during this time; stated people were annoying him; that they talked about him; said everyone was his enemy. At times became noisy and excited and made threats to kill his wife, whom, in presence of children, relatives and friends, he accused of misconduct with various men. Very vile in his language to wife and adult daughter; religiously fanatical. Wife refused to sign commitment papers and patient was discharged on contract to her custody.

Method

Mental. Following discharge from psychopathic ward patient was followed up and induced to come to clinic. Came only twice, as he feared physician and worker were in league with others to do him harm. Wife of patient endured his abuse for over a year after taking him from ward, and then asked worker to help her to have patient arrested on charge of non-support, as he had threatened to kill wife and children and they lived in fear of him. At court, after much difficulty due to refusal of judge to believe anything was wrong with patient mentally, he was again sent to psychopathic ward for observation. Committed to a state hospital where he remained for nine months. Upon being paroled, reported regularly to state hospital clinic, fearing he would be recommitted unless he did so. Attitude toward family changed and improved first month or two following home-coming.

Physical. Patient in good physical condition; arranged for treatment of certain physical ills of wife.

Social. Worker attempted on several occasions to obtain work for patient, but he refused proffered help. Obtained work by himself, and although wage offered was less than half the standard wage as set by union, patient refused to accept more than half of what was offered him, giving as an explanation that he did not need more for his personal wants. Worker went to see employer and arranged that balance of wages be sent direct to wife without patient being aware of this arrangement. Offered to advance patient money necessary to reinstate him in his union, but he refused offer. Family advised regarding various problems involved in dealing with patient.

Recreational. No cooperation from patient.

Result

Patient has shown but little improvement during two years he has been known to agency. No longer strikes wife and does not threaten to kill her, as he knows wife can and does come to agency and worker to help in dealing with him. Feels that if he misbehaves as formerly wife will have him rearrested and returned to state hospital. Family now have a better understanding as to how to deal with patient and have readjusted themselves to the needs of the situation.

GENERAL PARALYSIS

CASE 19

Diagnosis. General paralysis.

F. H. Negative.

P. H. Male; age 42; born in Russia; U. S. 15 years; watchmaker; married; wife and four children.

Psychosis. Patient admitted a specific, infection at age of 18 years; three years later complained of lightening pains in legs and body. At age of 41 years remained out of work for several months due to numerous somatic complaints. For a year had been more nervous and irritable than formerly, and had failed physically; complained of pains in region of heart and of general weariness; had no ambition to work and was depressed because hands were so tremulous that he could not hold a position. Taken to psychopathic ward and committed to a state hospital; there two months and paroled.

Method

Mental. Referred to clinic after discharge from state hospital, examined and advised regarding further treatment. Came to clinic thereafter at irregular intervals, coming particularly when he did not feel quite well.

Physical. Arranged for necessary treatment of patient at a general hospital. Wasserman tests taken of other members of family and found to be negative.

Social. Aided family with living expenses when necessary. Advanced sum of money to patient with which to buy a quantity of barber supplies; peddled same and for a period of five years has managed to earn enough to help family become totally self-supporting. Younger children sent to summer camp.

Recreational. Advised at clinic, though patient felt he needed but little since he was out in the open most of the day.

Result

Patient has not returned to a state hospital and has not deteriorated mentally, though he has shown but little improvement with advancing years.

ARTERIOSCLEROSIS

CASE 20

Diagnosis. Arteriosclerosis; organic nervous disease.

F. H. Unascertained.

P. H. Male; age 63; born in Russia; U. S. 40 years; no occupation; widower.

Psychosis. For several years patient disoriented; unable to give age to examining physician; nor date and place of birth; failed to recognize his children; at times very confused; became excited; wandered about; threatened to harm grandchildren.

Method

Mental. Patient brought to clinic by children for examination and advice as to what should be done, as they could not care for him because of his mental condition. Advised to commit patient to a state hospital as the only solution under the circumstances.

Physical. - - - - -

Social. No need.

Recreational. - - - - -

Result

Patient committed to a state hospital as was advised.

MENTAL DEFICIENCY

CASE 21

Diagnosis. Mentally inferior with hypomanic traits.

F. H. Father queer, deserted family number of years ago; mother paralyzed in lower limbs for about 15 years.

P. H. Male; age 15; born in U. S.; attended public school in ungraded classes.

Psychosis. Patient was a pupil in a truant school, and was sent to Children's Court by principal because of strange behavior; got into many fights with other pupils; would bring knives and slugs to school and cause much trouble. From court sent to psychopathic ward for observation where diagnosis was made. Returned to school with a reprimand from judge.

Method

Mental. After discharge from hospital followed-up and induced to come to clinic. Stated that at times he heard voices, became dizzy, was weak and frequently fell. No history of epilepsy could be discovered; patient was examined regularly at clinic and advised.

Physical. Condition good; well-developed for his years; no serious ailment found. Mother and ailing sister advised.

Social. Patient could not get along well with the principal and teachers in the school which he attended last. Obtained transfer to another truant school and did very well there during the few months he had to attend till his sixteenth birthday. Worker conferred with principals of both schools. Patient accounted for his bad behavior by stating his mother was very ill and poor and he wanted to go to work to help support her and a sick sister; thought by misbehaving would be given working papers and discharged from school. Advised and helped patient obtain proper employment; arranged for admission to a trade school.

Recreational. Helped patient plan his evening and spare-time activities; joined athletic group in public school center.

Result

At end of two years, working regularly as helper, salary $20.00 per week, all of which he gives to his mother. No longer complains of hearing voices; no dizzy spells. Hypomanic condition cleared up, though he is still mentally inferior.

HYSTERIA

CASE 22

Diagnosis. Hysteria.

F. H. Negative.

P. H. Female; age 33; born in Russia; U. S. 16 years; housework and embroiderer; deserted by husband; one child.

Psychosis. After a great deal of trouble with her husband he deserted her; shortly thereafter she suffered a physical breakdown. At that time, *i. e.*, three years before being referred to mental hygiene agency, doctors told her she had heart trouble and advised her not to exert herself unduly. Went to bed and did not rise for three years, fearing she would die if she exerted herself. Taken to a general hospital, remained there five weeks, transferred to psychopathic ward, and taken home next day by relatives.

Method

Mental. After discharge from psychopathic ward, patient visited by mental hygiene worker. Since patient could not leave the house, psychiatrist visited her at home. Worker visited patient almost daily for several months; through much coaxing and persuasion, patient was induced to do things she had formerly feared because of her supposed heart condition; gotten out of bed and made to sit in a chair; later walked a few steps; gradually began to dress and care for self; taken down to street and for automobile rides until she finally gained sufficient confidence in herself to walk home from where she had been left, several blocks from her home.

Physical. Physician brought to patient for physical examinations; taken to hospital for X-ray of lungs, which were found to be negative for tuberculosis, of which there had been a suspicion; treated for her minor cardiac condition, both at home and in hospital. Confidence restored in learning that there was nothing seriously the matter with her.

Social. Family aided financially so that patient might be sent to seashore for bathing and convalescence. Family educated in proper care of patient.

Recreational. Walks with worker; automobile rides; ocean bathing.

Result

After being under care for one year, patient entirely recovered mentally and much improved physically. Members of family and neighbors think a miracle was achieved.

CONSTITUTIONAL PSYCHOPATHIC INFERIORITY

Case 23

Diagnosis. Constitutional psychopathic inferiority with depressed episodes.

F. H. Negative; father many years older than mother.

P. H. Female; age 19; born in Russia; U. S. 3 years; factory worker; single; three adult brothers in city.

Psychosis. Patient became depressed because of loss of position and attempted suicide by drinking carbolic acid; taken to psychopathic ward; remained there a few days and was discharged. Within a week again attempted suicide by drinking iodine; returned to psychopathic ward and committed to a state hospital, where she was detained two months. Shortly after discharge, threatened on several occasions to commit suicide and to kill several persons known to her. Often became drunk. Attempts to have her committed again unsuccessful, as brothers refused to sign commitment papers and physicians on psychopathic ward refused to admit her unless papers were first signed.

Method

Mental. Following discharge from state hospital patient came to clinic at irregular intervals for about four years. Advised by physician about her depressions, *etc.* Social worker spent much time with patient, helping her over her periods of depression and trying to give her a new outlook on life. During examination at clinic stated, "I heard voices when I was in the convalescent home because it was very quiet there. I was afraid to sleep—I imagined I saw things and heard voices in my head. Sometimes I heard someone walking—I was afraid to be there—I was nervous."

Physical. Patient taken to physicians and hospitals for examination and treatment of various ailments complained of by her. For a long time insisted she had some gynecological difficulty; examinations by women physicians failed to discover anything. Sent to convalescent home when rundown physically.

Social. When patient was out of work, home found for her and board and incidentals paid for by agency. Suitable employment found for patient; sent to trade school; given English lessons at home by worker, as patient complained that lack of sufficient knowledge of language caused her much worry. Visited places of employment and interested employers in patient.

Recreational. Taken for walks to places of amusement; given tickets to concerts; interested in club work.

Result

Despite all attempts of physician and worker to help patient, she persisted in drinking, going to cabarets with chance acquaintances, painting, dressing in a vulgar way, *etc*. Worker could not obtain cooperation of brothers when it was seen that she was heading towards a life of immorality, as they persistently refused to sign commitment papers. During periods of depression, patient would come to office of agency in a drunken condition, create a disturbance, and threaten to kill several of the workers. Admitted she was leading an immoral life, but nothing could be done by worker to have her committed because of attitude of brothers and of physician in psychopathic ward. Was finally arrested for soliciting on the streets and sent to Bedford Reformatory for three years.

Case 24

Diagnosis. Constitutional psychopathic inferiority with episodes of excitement.

F. H. Father nervous and irritable.

P. H. Male; age 18; born in U. S.; clerical worker.

Psychosis. For six months prior to admission of patient to psychopathic ward, he showed an inability to get along with his parents and brothers, with spells of irritability; lacked efficiency at work. On ward was emotionally unstable, with some depression; had considerable insight into his condition which he ascribed to excessive masturbation.

Method

Mental. Patient was committed to a state hospital, as his parents insisted they could not cope with him. Remained in hospital for eight months, was well-behaved and occupied as a messenger about the institution. After discharge referred to clinic; found to have improved while in hospital; advised regarding personal habits, *etc.* Within a few weeks parents returned patient to hospital, complaining he had again become irritable and unable to get along at home. Paroled within a few weeks; in about two months returned to hospital of own accord; sent to city on an errand and failed to return to hospital. Came to clinic and showed some signs of improvement, though unusually talkative. Returned to hospital of his own accord within a few months, as he felt better there than at home. Though hospital physicians were willing to discharge him within a few weeks after last admission and patient requested his discharge, parents refused to take him home until he was in a much better condition mentally.

Physical. Prescribed at clinic for slight physical ailment.

Social. Obtained employment for patient when he was out on parole from hospital. Main effort was to educate parents to a proper understanding of the patient and how to care for and treat him when he was at home.

Recreational. Advised regarding suitable forms of recreation.

Result

Patient has had to return to and remain in the state hospital because of inability of parents to understand and care for him during periods when he was irritable. Lack of cooperation of parents largely responsible for hospital residence of patient. Poor, dirty home in a crowded tenement district contributing factor to irritability of patient. Could not induce parents to move to a better neighborhood for sake of patient, as father had business interests which he felt he could not sacrifice. Impossible to obtain cooperation of parents to have patient boarded in a better district and home. Necessary to wait until patient becomes older and his earning capacity will increase sufficient to render it possible for him to be entirely self-supporting when living away from home.

CASE 25

Diagnosis. Constitutional psychopathic inferiority.

F. H. Unascertained.

P. H. Female; age 20; born in U. S.; typist; unmarried mother with one child; seduced at 18 years by an Italian. Following death of father, sent to orphan asylum at age of ten years.

Psychosis. Showed kleptomaniac tendencies at orphan asylum; after discharge at age of fifteen consorted with gang of thieves, acting as female accomplice. Finally arrested, sent to City Prison to await trial; actions and behavior caused transfer to psychopathic ward for observation and examination; found that she was not a committable case though subject to mild disturbances of short duration. Paroled by court and referred to mental hygiene agency.

Method

Mental. Examined at clinic regularly and advised.

Physical. Needs attended to.

Social. Given clerical work; board paid as long as was necessary; clothing provided; baby boarded with its father's relatives; worker saw patient regularly for two years and at intervals for several years thereafter; obtained a stenographic position.

Recreational. Advised very carefully.

Result

Patient has had a regular position for several years as stenographer in the government service, salary $1200 per year; pays board for child, of which she is very fond. Consistently refuses to marry father of the child; has had no difficulties for several years; thoroughly adjusted.

The presentation of these twenty-five cases, even though

in outline form only, should give to the reader a comparatively fair conception of the problems that are faced by physicians and social workers in the clinics of an organization specializing in the social service side of mental hygiene activities. The various combinations of circumstances, though numerous as far as these few cases are concerned, do not exhaust the wide range of possible problems that arise in dealing with mental hygiene patients. The attempt has been not to present selected and chosen cases, but rather to indicate as far as possible what amounts to a cross-section of the work in its various phases. Lack of space alone prohibits the presentation of one hundred or more cases, in each of which a particular set of problems need solution. Every mental patient and his family are the source of a new group of difficulties; and although certain of these can be pigeonholed as it were, still each patient must be studied separately, a plan for serving prepared and without hesitation modified as the exigencies of the developing situations demand.

CHAPTER VI

Recommendations and Conclusion

I. SHORTCOMINGS OF SOCIAL SERVICE

The activities of most social service agencies depend for their efficacy and sphere of influence for good in a community upon the funds available from year to year, upon the personnel, the equipment with which they have to work, and the moral support of the socially minded persons whose interest is aroused in their work. This is as true of a mental hygiene as of any other agency. In a large community like New York City, there is never a dearth of patients; the problem is rather to obtain sufficient funds to maintain clinics in different parts of the greater city and to render both medical and social service of a high order.

From the cases cited in the preceding chapter it was seen that, at least with some types of patients, such as those afflicted with manic depressive insanity, much can be accomplished and the patients saved from commitment to a state hospital for the insane. Social service has been less successful with cases of dementia praecox, general paralysis, paranoid conditions, psychoneuroses and others. This lack of success corresponds to the failure of the state hospitals to improve the mental condition of patients similarly diagnosed. From one point of view, however, this comparison is not altogether justified. Social service with mental cases aims to achieve just what state hospitals have thus far failed to accomplish; if, therefore, psychiatric social work is to develop upon a firm basis it must prove its utility as an important and distinct factor in increasing the ratio of recoveries and eventually decreasing the incidence of insanity and psychoneuroses.

II. NEED OF A NEWER METHOD OF APPROACH TO PROBLEM

While it is true that social service, as at present organized, functions most satisfactorily with cases of manic depressive insanity, it must be recognized that psychiatric social work has been largely limited to treating and caring for acute, chronic and occasionally borderline cases, and that the much broader field of prevention has in the main been neglected. Why this should be so is quite understandable. The attention of the public, of the legislatures, and of physicians has been absorbed in providing suitable places of confinement for those who have already shown symptoms of mental disease; and, as has been repeatedly pointed out, even this phase of the problem is still far from being adequately met.

During the past few years, particularly since the development of the mental hygiene movement, it has become more and more apparent that one of the chief reasons for the low percentage of recovery and improvement has been the circumstance that those ailing mentally are not reached soon enough either by mental hygiene clinics or by the state hospitals. Only in cases of acute attacks are the patients given early care and treatment; where the onset of the disease is gradual and spread over weeks or months, the patient too often comes to the attention of the specialist in mental diseases when nothing but state hospital care can be recommended.

The implications of these facts are obvious, and if we are to achieve greater success in helping those who are headed towards the state hospital for the insane, we must begin to attack the problem in a different way. Maintaining clinics for the mentally sick, psychiatric social work, state hospitals for the insane, psychopathic hospitals, and other agencies that are called upon to help meet the problems that arise, are one and all essential in a program aiming to conserve the mental health of a community. But the goal to be sought by all who are interested in the problem of insanity should be a gradual decrease in the number of persons whom it is found necessary to commit to state hospitals and similar institutions. Instead of striving to obtain larger and still larger appropriations for additional state hospital accommodations, as is unfortunately being done at the present time, ordinary prudence would indicate that some other or additional action was necessary to limit the ever increasing need to maintain in comparative indolence thousands of persons who have or will become mentally ill.

III. MENTAL HYGIENE AND CHILDHOOD

From the point of view of mental hygiene, individuals may be said to fall into one of the following groups: (a) those now sane, and who will remain sane except through the working of some exogenous factor; (b) those now sane, but who will become insane under certain conditions; (c) those now insane; (d) those who have been insane but who are now recovered and have returned to the community. To this might be added a fifth group—those yet unborn.[1] From this it is seen that those who belong to the first two groups, whether children or adults, may, under certain unfavorable conditions, come in time to be a part of groups (c) and (d). Our chief problem is how to prevent this from coming about, particularly insofar as the children are concerned.

Students of psychiatry have come to realize more and more that the patients whom they have observed in hos-

[1] Williams, Frankwood E., "Psychopathic Hospitals and Prophylaxis," *Boston Med. and Surg. Jour.*, June 24, 1915, p. 933.

pitals for the insane and elsewhere were in need of special study and care as children, and that it was the duty of society to have discovered their special needs and to have given them the attention which their future welfare demanded.[1] Viewing the matter from the basis of our present knowledge, we may be inclined to forgive the failings of a generation ago, though an enlightened public opinion is to-day demanding that preventive measures be taken early enough in the lives of children to discover and when possible to correct, faulty habits of mind and action which in later life may result in the development of some neurosis or psychosis. A program which would show definite results would of necessity have to concern itself with children of a very early age. A plan prepared by Prof. Arnold Gesell of Yale University for the complete examination of children includes the following measures, which would be particularly applicable to a large city, though likewise adjustable to rural and village conditions:[2]

(a) A hygienic supervision of the pre-school period. This to result in a cumulative biographic record of every child from birth registration to school entrance.

(b) A psycho-physical entrance examination of every school beginner. This examination should be comprehensive, thoroughgoing and in close cooperation with parent or guardian; it should also summarize the main conclusions from the pre-school career of the child and disclose those children either superior or atypical who most urgently need a specialized school career.

(c) A reorganization of the kindergarten and first year, which will place the first half year of school life under systematic, purposeful observation.

[1] Yerkes, Robert M., "How We May Discover Children Who Need Special Care," *Mental Hygiene*, April, 1917, p. 252.

[2] Gesell, Arnold, "Mental Hygiene and the Public School," *Mental Hygiene*, Jan., 1919, pp. 4-10.

(d) The development of a new type of school nurse, who by supervision, corrective teaching, and home visiting, will further the concrete everyday tasks of mental hygiene. Her problems would be children with night terrors, the nail biter, the over tearful child, the over silent child, the stammering child, the extremely indifferent child, the pervert, the infantile child, the unstable choreic, and a whole host of suffering, frustrated and unhealthily constituted growing minds, that we are barely aware of in a quantitative sense, because we do not have the agencies to bring them to our attention as problems of public hygiene and prophylaxis.

(e) The development of reconstruction schools, of special classes and vacation camps for certain groups of children who need specialized treatment, such as the speech defective, psychopathic and nervous groups. To such schools, classes and camps, children could be assigned for long or short periods, and secure a combination of medical and educational treatment which alone is adequate to reconstruct them mentally. These provisions imply neurological and psychiatric specialists, educational psychologists and teacher-nurses, cooperating as public health experts in a work of mental salvage and prophylaxis.

Only by such radical and sincere methods can we ever hope to reduce the massive burden of adult insanity. Expensive in the beginning, a preventive juvenile system of mental sanitation may after all prove to be a form of socialized thrift.

IV. MENTAL HYGIENE AND ADOLESCENCE

Adolescence is generally recognized as a critical period in the mental life of the individual. Not only is it a period during which disorders are very apt to develop, but it is also a time when the mental balance of probably every boy and girl is disturbed to a greater or lesser degree. In fact, many of the breaks, perhaps most of them, occur in the adolescent period or the period of early adulthood.[1] The disturbance is shown in a variety of ways, as for example, by a tendency to become irritable and discontented or to indulge in day-dreams and romantic fancies. The changes in behavior and disposition which young people display at that time frequently make them difficult to deal with and cause a great deal of trouble and worry to those who are responsible for their care and upbringing.

Emphasis has already been placed upon the need for the early recognition of latent or active mental disorders; and upon the fact that approximately sixty per cent of the patients in the state hospitals in New York State have been diagnosed as cases of dementia praecox, with a history, following the age of puberty, of inability for healthy mental adjustment. In these patients, the inability to adjust themselves resulted in unwholesome habits of thought and conduct, in bad sexual practices or antisocial acts, and in certain types of mental reactions usually regarded as manifestations of mental disease.

In preventing the development of these unhealthy types of mental adjustment during the adolescent period, there is a very important field of work and one in which very little has as yet been done. There are few boys or girls who would not be the better for some assistance and guidance during the adolescent period. There are many with whom it would make all the difference between becoming useful members of society and permanent inmates of institutions. The time to deal with these disorders and difficulties of adjustment is just as soon as they appear, though the pre-

[1] White, William A., "Childhood: the Golden Period for Mental Hygiene," *Mental Hygiene*, Apr., 1920, p. 266.

liminary training should be initiated long before in order to inhibit their later development. The adolescent boy or girl should be helped to make a wholesome adjustment to the demands of his instinctive nature in the first place, for by the time he reaches a hospital for the insane, he has commonly departed so far from normal habits of thought and conduct that attempts to reeducate him are of very little use.[1] There must be psychiatrists in the upper grades of the public schools and in the high schools, for frequently it is there that incipient mental disorder first shows itself. There must be more mental hygiene clinics and education of the public in regard to the subject of mental hygiene.

It may be interesting to note at this point that the mental hygiene division of the Free Synagogue, of which mention has already been made, has established and maintains a country home or camp to which are sent adolescent girls recommended by physicians, nurses, teachers, social service agencies and others. The girls are examined by a psychiatrist and if found to be cases of mental maladjustment in danger of developing some mental or nervous disorder, they are sent to the camp for a period of several weeks or even months. While there they are under the constant and direct supervision of a nurse specially trained in work with this type of girl. They are followed-up after discharge, hold reunions throughout the fall and winter, and in case of further need of country care are permitted to return to the camp until their condition has shown marked improvement. The experiment has well justified the expense involved and raises the hope that similar camps or convalescent homes for other groups will prove to be a very effective means of preventing mental and nervous breakdowns in later life.

[1] Harrington, Milton A., "Mental Disorder in Adolescence," *Mental Hygiene*, Apr., 1920, p. 379.

V. MENTAL HYGIENE NEEDS OF A COMMUNITY

The object of this study having been largely limited to a consideration of the social aspects of the treatment of the insane, it may be worth while to point out in closing, the fundamental items of a mental hygiene program for a community, taking for granted that the thoughts already expressed, particularly upon the problem of the child and the adolescent, do not need reiteration.

Mental hygiene activities, as will be remembered, aimed first of all to educate the mass of people regarding the essentials of proper nervous and mental life. Following this came the establishment of mental hygiene clinics with their psychiatrists and specially trained social workers. The plan of activities of certain mental hygiene clinics operating in New York City was presented in the preceding chapter and it was implied that the equipment of the mental hygiene agency operating these clinics is by no means adequate to meet the pressing needs. It is not merely a question of inadequate financial resources to establish more clinics in different parts of the city; other fundamentals are lacking to round out the activities and power for service to the community. A presentation of these will go a considerable way toward indicating what the minimum facilities should be in every large community in order to meet the mental hygiene requirements.

First of all we can proceed on the assumption that in any given community the mental hygiene facilities are not adequate to serve those in pressing need of this kind of medical attention. There is not a city of any size where sufficient emphasis is being placed upon the mental health of the population, either through the activities of the public institutions and their officers, by private agencies, or a combination of both. The fact of the matter is that the mental hygiene idea is only beginning to take root in various sections of the country. It will be some time before an awakened and aroused public conscience takes recognition of its needs, spurred, perhaps, by the propaganda and stimulation of local societies for mental hygiene or by the National Committee for Mental Hygiene.

It should again be made plain that, as at present organized, state hospitals are not prepared to meet the mental hygiene needs of a community without the active assistance and financial support of private organizations. By this is meant that the private agencies should cooperate with and supplement the work of the state hospitals by various activities, some of which will be explained in the following section.

VI. MENTAL HYGIENE AGENCIES

At least four elements are necessary to the proper organization of a mental hygiene agency. These are (a) clinics; (b) convalescent homes; (c) a model factory or workshop; and (d) a psychiatric institute functioning in conjunction with the other items in the program.

(a) *Clinics.* Clinic organization and plan of service have already been discussed and will be passed over at this point, except to note the further suggestion that before the establishment of any clinics in a community a survey should be made of the distribution of the population that is most likely to come to these mental hygiene clinics. Moreover, whenever possible, such clinics should be established within the buildings of a general hospital. With the development of hospitals as health centers, it seems most advisable that mental hygiene clinics should also become part of the community health program.

(b) *Convalescent Homes.* Those engaged in psychiatric social work often feel themselves at a loss as to where to send a mental case in need of convalescent care. It may be of interest to note that there is hardly a convalescent home or institution in or near New York City at present that will accept as an inmate one who has been discharged from a state hospital and is in need of a temporary change of environment or convalescent care. The only institution approximating such a place which receives mental cases is the camp already mentioned, and to which, because of lack of room, only adolescent girls are admitted. As a result of this state of affairs, early mental cases and those verging upon a breakdown must be committed to state hospitals from which they might otherwise be saved, or they must be sent to private sanatoria, where the standard of care and attention is often inferior. In the case of single persons without any immediate relatives or friends in the community, the attempt has to be made at an early stage to board them in selected private homes. None of these expedients has as yet been found satisfactory. The only solution that seems at all feasible is the establishment of one or more convalescent homes specializing in the care of mental cases. These might be similar to the institutions already in existence to which are sent persons in danger of a physical breakdown, or those recuperating from surgical operations and severe physical ailments.

(c) *Workshop for Mental Hygiene Patients.* From a reading of the cases cited in the preceding chapter it must have been realized that one of the main difficulties faced in trying to assist patients to readjust themselves was the inability to provide suitable employment for them under favorable working conditions. It is not very difficult to find some kind of work when there is a labor shortage, but the problem is so to place mental hygiene patients that for one reason or another they will not feel compelled to leave the job found for them within a few hours or days after beginning work. The difficulty is that these persons cannot fit into what we to-day call, whether rightly or wrongly, the normal industrial life. They must have working conditions specially planned to meet their particular needs. Thus, the recovered and improved cases of manic depressive insanity find it well-nigh impossible to return to former sweatshop and high-speed industrial life without exposing themselves to a relapse and readmission to the state hospital. The numerous early cases of dementia praecox and others lose one position after another because the employer does not understand and refuses to sympathize with their condition and discharges them when they repeatedly come late in the morning, when they feel indisposed and remain away from work, and otherwise fail to measure up to the standard and pace set by their healthy fellow-workers.

Suitable occupation under favorable conditions is an established and recognized therapeutic agent for mental cases. To prevent the numerous relapses and hospital readmissions. as well as to stave off, in the first place, the need for commitment because of social maladjustment arising from industrial and occupational difficulties, model workshops for mental hygiene patients should be established. A workshop for Jewish men and women afflicted with tuberculosis has for several years been in operation in New York City under the direction of a social agency. The project long ago outgrew the experimental stage and has from its inception been a successful venture from the social, medical, occupational and economic viewpoints. The same kind of workshop, with certain necessary modifications, should be established for mental hygiene patients. It would then not be necessary for patients discharged from state hospitals to reenter at once the industry which in the first place contributed to their mental or nervous breakdown. Those suffering from the milder forms of mental disease could find gainful occupation where they would work under the supervision of those who understood their condition, and where they would not be compelled to work when they were not well. The establishment of such an industrial unit or center would indeed be a landmark in the development of the health conscience of the community, and in the progress of the mental hygiene movement.

(d) *Psychopathic Hospital.* The fourth element necessary to round out the program of work of a mental hygiene organization is a psychopathic hospital, to which might be admitted for observation and treatment cases of mild mental disturbance otherwise destined to go about neglected until they finally had to be sent to a state hospital. The need for such an institution is particularly apparent in a large cosmopolitan city like New York, with its thousands of admissions annually to the psychopathic wards of general hospitals, from which but comparatively few are discharged except to a state hospital. Such an institution as proposed would be in a position to treat patients long before they were in need of state hospital care, and only such patients as it was possible to help to mental health within a comparatively short time would be admitted for treatment.

The question of the utility of psychopathic or reception hospitals has been discussed elsewhere and will not be reopened. It is sufficient to state that in large communities such an institution is essential to a complete plan for the early care and treatment of mental and nervous cases, and that the work and results of the Boston Psychopathic Hospital as well as of the Phipps Institute in Baltimore have completely justified the hopes of the original sponsors of the idea.

It is felt by many students of the problem in New York City, that, due to the large Jewish population in New York, as well as to the peculiar psychology of the Jew and more especially of the recent immigrants among the Jews, it would be advisable to plan and erect a Jewish psychopathic hospital or institute, either as an independent unit or as a part of an already established general or special hospital. The organization of a committee representative of various elements of the community and interested primarily in preventive and reconstructive work along lines of mental hygiene, and the establishment of clinics, convalescent homes, workshops, and a psychopathic hospital, would be a great step forward in mental hygiene and psychiatric social work. Such a group has already been formed among the Jews of New York, but its efforts are still in their infancy. The plan outlined for a community program is applicable to any city, though it would have to be modified somewhat to meet local conditions.

VII. CONCLUSION

In attempting to point out and discuss the social aspects of the treatment of the insane, the primary aim of the writer has been to bring before those who are vitally interested in the whole and baffling question of insanity, whether from the viewpoint of the physician, minister, social worker or layman, facts which will lead to a better understanding of the various phases of the problem. The presentation of the development of legislation affecting the insane in New York State in the first chapter was intended as a background upon which to picture the other aspects which were later considered, for much of the care and treatment of the insane is integrally related to the question of legislation. The three subsequent chapters presented, first, the patient before coming to and while in the psychopathic ward of a general hospital as well as the disposition of such patients; second, the patient in the state hospital to which he was transferred from the psychopathic ward, and his disposition by the state hospital; and third, the patient after leaving the state hospital. These three chapters indicated what the city and state were doing for the insane who came under their care. The fifth chapter portrayed the activities of a privately supported social agency specializing in mental hygiene activities. The recommendations of the final chapter point out the lines the newer work for mental cases will have to follow in order to achieve a higher degree of success in preventing and curing insanity, With the public aroused to a deeper interest in all that pertains to the insane, improved methods of treating mental disorders would develop apace.

INDEX

VITA

Jacob Alter Goldberg, born in New York City, June 10, 1890. Educated in New York City public schools; graduated Townsend Harris High School; College of the City of New York, A.B., February, 1913. Entered Columbia University in September, 1914, as a graduate student under the Faculty of Political Science; received A.M. degree June, 1916; title of essay submitted for master's degree: *Drug Addiction as a Social and Legislative Problem.* Continued at Columbia University to Jan. 1921. Special student Union Theological Seminary, 1916-1917. For a number of years in charge of a social settlement; taught in the evening schools; district supervisor of lectures; inspector of dance halls, theatres, *etc.*; hospital social service worker; associated with Drs. Stephen S. Wise and Sidney E. Goldstein in the religious, social and educational work of the Free Synagogue. Since 1917, secretary of the mental hygiene division, social service department, Free Synagogue. At Columbia University studied under Profs. Lindsay, Devine, Giddings, Seager, Barnett, and Chaddock.

www.ingramcontent.com/pod-product-compliance
Lightning Source LLC
LaVergne TN
LVHW020056110826
845151LV00005B/1492
9781425523541